A GREAT WEEKEND IN

MADRID

A GREAT WEEKEND IN
MADRID

In constant competition with its rival Barcelona, Madrid became the capital of Spain in 1561 when Felipe II chose to establish his court here and made the city the seat of government and administration. Since then, '*Sólo Madrid es Corte*' (the only court is Madrid), though the city is far from being solely a reflection of its royal past.

The Madrid of the royal Habsburg dynasty can still be found in the old city centre where the narrow streets and alleyways are home to modest shops where you can watch traditional craftsmen at work. These densely-woven districts open via narrow passageways onto the celebrated Plaza Mayor, the vast 17th-century square, lined with cafés and craft shops. Nearby, the Plaza de Santa Ana, with its bars and theatres, is just as lively by night as by day. Also close is Puerta del Sol ('gateway of the sun'), one of Madrid's most popular meeting places where people meet up with friends to catch up on all the latest news. Built in the shape of a crescent, this square is considered to be the starting point of all the roads in Spain, and it forms the very heart of the city. Madrid is also home to the *paseo*, the broad avenue that crosses the city from north to south. It comprises several parts. The oldest, the Paseo del Prado, was built in the 18th century by Carlos III, the 'enlightened' king. It then changes its name to the Paseo de Recoletos and finally becomes the Paseo de la Castellana. As soon as the weather turns fine, its shady walks, ornamental gardens and terraces become the haunt of Madrid's café society, and the Paseo de la Castellana turns into the 'Costa Castellana'. The Parque del Retiro (Retiro Park) is a must if you like

Pedro Almodóvar believes, but the city remains a favourite haunt of night-owls. Try to adopt the Spanish rhythm of life and you can enjoy it yourself. Start your evenings in the tapas bars with a bite of *tortilla* washed down with a glass of Rioja. Move on and dance the night away in one of the many fashionable clubs and end your night in the small hours over a cup of hot chocolate and *churros*. When you set out on your evening in Madrid,

sport and walking. Madrid is a haven for art lovers too. The city is home to many works of art and the museums, royal palace and churches are simply breathtaking. The incomparable collection of paintings by El Greco, Goya, Velázquez, Murillo, Picasso and many others will hold you spellbound for hours. All these treasures of the past should not let us forget that Madrid is also a city looking towards the future. This can be witnessed in the high number of artists and designers living and working here. The death of Franco in 1975 launched a new period of artistic and personal liberty, known as the *Movida* ('the action'), in the Spanish capital. The new, emancipated generation found the freedom to stay out to the early hours, drinking and partying, revolutionising the city's cultural and artistic life, which had been stifled for too long. The *Movida* may be just a distant memory, as its leading light, cult film director

wear your latest finds from the trendy boutiques. You're sure to be *a la ultima* (dressed in the height of fashion). Yet nostalgia and tradition still find a place in the Madrid of the third millennium. Bullfighting is as popular as ever and Las Ventas bullring draws capacity crowds for every *corrida*. *Zarzuela* (operetta), which had once become the preserve of the city's older inhabitants has again found a faithful following. The *manolos* in their traditional costumes still dance the *chotis* to the sound of a pianola. Last but not least, the *verbenas*, the famous popular festivals, still draw an impressive crowd of *Madrileños* (the inhabitants of Madrid), who wouldn't miss these age-old celebrations for the world.

How to get there

The Spanish have a saying 'freeze for nine months, bake for three' which just about sums up the climate of Madrid. It may seem a little exaggerated, but it shouldn't be taken too lightly either.

THE CLIMATE

At an altitude of 600m (2,000ft), Madrid winters are harsh and dry and it isn't unusual for the thermometer to fall below zero. In July and August the stifling heat can send temperatures soaring above 40°C (104°F), making life in the city almost unbearable. The rest of the year the temperature is ideal and there are many sunny days. October, February, March and April are mild, pleasant months and May and June ideal times of year for walking in the centre of the city and discovering its varied nightlife.

HOW TO GET THERE

If you're planning a short stay, it's better to go by train or plane. You can get big reductions by booking well in advance.

FLIGHTS FROM THE UK

British Airways
☎ 0345 222 111
www.britishairways.com
Offers several daily flights direct from London Gatwick.

British Midland
☎ 0870 607 0555
www.flybmi.com
Direct daily flight from London Heathrow.

Easyjet
☎ 0870 6000 000
www.easyjet.com
Direct daily flights from Luton airport.

Iberia
☎ 020 7830 0011
Daily direct flights from London Heathrow and one daily flight from Manchester.

FROM IRELAND

Aerlingus
☎ 01 886 8888
www.aerlingus.com
Offers direct flights to Madrid from Dublin twice a week. Flights from other cities in Ireland go via Dublin.

British Airways
☎ 1800 626 747
www.britishairways.com
Daily flights from Shannon, Cork and Dublin via London Gatwick.

Iberia
☎ 01 407 3017
One direct daily flight from Dublin. Flights from other cities in Ireland go via Dublin.

FROM THE USA AND CANADA

British Airways
☎ 1-800-AIRWAYS
www.britishairways.com
Daily flights via London from many US and Canadian cities.

Continental
☎ 800 231 0856
www.continental.com
Direct daily flights from
Newark, USA.

Delta
☎ 800 241 4141
Direct daily flights from
Atlanta and New York JFK.

Iberia
☎ 800 772 4642
Direct daily flights from
New York, Miami and Los
Angeles as well as Toronto
and Montreal.

FROM AUSTRALIA AND NEW ZEALAND

There are no direct flights
from Australia or New
Zealand to Madrid. Singapore
Airlines (☎ 02 9350 0100;
www.singaporeair.com) fly
via Singapore and British
Airways (☎ 02 8904 8800;
www.britishairways.com) fly
via London. Check with your
travel agent for the easiest
and most economical route.

BY TRAIN

It's a good idea to travel by
train if you're on a tight
budget. Trains from northern
European destinations arrive
at the Estación de Charmatín
in the north of the city. If
you're travelling from the
south or east of Spain, you'll
arrive at the Estación de
Atocha. Trains from local
towns around Madrid arrive at
the Estacion del Norte, which
is close to the centre near the
Palacio Real.

It's a long journey from the
UK and Ireland and you'll
need to allow at least 20
hours. If you decide to go by
train your trip will, of course,
include crossing the English
Channel, which you can do by
ferry or by taking the Eurostar
(☎ 0990 186 186) to Paris.
From there you can take the
overnight sleeper service. The
journey takes about 14 hours
and you should enquire at
one of the train services listed
about this service.

European Rail
☎ 020 7387 0444 (UK)
www.europeanrail.co.uk

The International Rail Centre
☎ 0990 848 848 (UK)

You can also ask your travel
agent for more information.
If you require information
about rail services within
Spain, call the national rail
operator RENFE on ☎ 93 490
02 02 (domestic) or ☎ 93
490 11 22 (international).

INCLUSIVE BREAKS

Many tour operators offer
two and three-day weekend
breaks that include travel
(by plane, train or coach) and
accommodation in various
categories of hotel. The main
advantage of these breaks is
that they give you the chance
to stay at a luxury hotel for a
very reasonable price. You
also benefit from the rates
negotiated by tour operators
and travel more cheaply while
avoiding the bother of
booking. However, the choice
of hotels is often limited and
they generally belong to big
hotel chains. It's better to
avoid them if you
want a small,
charming hotel.

Weekend breaks to Madrid from the UK can be booked through the following agents:

Bridge Travel Service
☎ 01233 214124 (brochure),
☎ 01992 456600 (booking)

British Airways Holidays
☎ 0870 2424 243

Paradors of Spain
www.parador.es
☎ 91 516 6666 (Spain)

Or you can book through:

Keytel International (UK)
☎ 020 7616 0300 or
☎ 020 7402 8182
Email: Paradors@keytel.co.uk

Estancias de Espana
(historic accommodation)
www.estanciases.es or call your local Spanish Tourist Office.

INSURANCE

UK tour operators are obliged by law to offer insurance, but it varies from company to company. You may find you are covered against theft, health problems and repatriation but not loss of luggage or cancellation. Before buying additional travel insurance, check your home, car and medical policies, as well as any cover provided by credit card companies, and always use a reputable, well-known insurer.

City Escapades
☎ 0990 437 227 (brochure),
☎ 020 8748 2661 (booking)

Sovereign
☎ 0870 2430 635 (brochure),
☎ 0870 5768 373 (booking)

BOOKING A HOTEL

If you decide to arrange your stay yourself, you can contact the following organisations. They offer a wide choice of accommodation to suit all budgets and take care of the booking formalities for you.

Information about hotels and booking is available on:
☎ 902 202 202 (Spain)

SPANISH TOURIST OFFICES WORLDWIDE

UK & Ireland
22-23 Manchester Square
London
W1M 5AP
☎ 020 7486 8077

USA
666, 5th Avenue
35th floor
New York
NY 10103
☎ 212 265 8822

845 North Michigan Avenue
Chicago
IL 60611
☎ 312 642 1992

1221 Brickell Avenue
Suite 1850
Miami
FL 33131
☎ 305 358 1992

Canada
2 Bloor Streer West
34th Floor
Toronto, Ontario
M4W3EZ
☎ 416 961 3131

Australia and New Zealand
c/o Spanish Tourism Promotions
178 Collins Street
Melbourne
☎ 03 9650 7377

CUSTOMS

Spain is a signatory of the Schengen agreement, so European Union citizens no longer have to pass through customs on arrival. All you need is your passport. There's no limit on the amount and value of goods you can buy for your personal use and there are no customs formalities to complete on leaving Spain. The only exceptions to the rule are mail-order goods and new cars. For more information, contact your nearest international airport.

ENTRY REQUIREMENTS

Citizens of the European Union, including children under 16, must have a valid identity card or passport. Citizens of other countries may also require a visa. Contact your consulate or the Spanish consulate in the UK.

FROM THE AIRPORT TO THE CITY CENTRE

Madrid airport is situated north-east of the city around half an hour from the city centre, depending on the traffic. The best way to get to the centre is by taxi, but only take an official taxi (white with a red stripe) and make sure the driver starts the meter.

Taxis are relatively cheap (€12-15 depending on the location of your hotel and the number of pieces of luggage).

The metro also runs from the airport (Barajas) and buses run between the airport and the city centre every 12 minutes from 6am to 2am. They set you down in Plaza Colón.

FROM THE STATION TO THE CITY CENTRE

If you arrive by train, your first port-of-call in Madrid will be Chamartín station. To get to the centre, there's a choice of underground (line 8, Fuencarral-Nuevos Ministerios), bus or taxi. If you have to pick up a car, there's a shuttle to take you to the car park.

Chamartín Station
☎ 91 328 90 20

HIRING A CAR

You can easily reserve a car before your departure. Most of the major car hire companies can be found in the airport and station.

Avis
☎ 91 393 72 22

Budget
☎ 91 393 72 18

Europcar
☎ 91 393 72 89

Hertz
☎ 91 393 72 28

Expect to pay around €36 for two days hire of the cheapest (Corsa-type) category of car.

Driving in the city centre can be frustrating and there are often traffic jams. You are probably better off without a car, unless you want to make excursions to visit the surrounding area (El Escorial, for example). When it comes to parking, try to get into the underground car parks as early as possible and be very careful where you park. Until recently cars were hardly ever taken to the pound, but the authorities now seem to have taken a tougher attitude.

VOLTAGE

The electric current in Spain is 220 volts, as in most of mainland Europe. Plugs have two round pins and you may need to use an adaptor. It's a good idea to bring one with you if you want to be sure of being able to use your electric hair dryer or razor during your stay.

CURRENCY AND CASH

Spain is one of the EU members that joined the single currency, so in 2002 the euro replaced the peseta as legal tender. The euro, which is divided into 100 cents, has a fixed exchange rate of 166.386 pesetas to 1 euro.

You can change your money before you leave but you'll find full money-changing facilities when you arrive at the airport or station. In the city centre, there are plenty of cash machines that take international credit cards. Bureaux de change can be found in the vicinity of most tourist attractions, department stores and big hotels. You can change currency and traveller's cheques at all banks, but most are only open Monday to Friday, from 8.30am to 2pm. Some are also open until 1pm on Saturday.

BUDGETING

While Madrid is cheaper than some other European capitals, you certainly can't live here for next to nothing.

You need to allow around €255 a day per couple for meals, snacks, outings,

---

USEFUL NUMBERS IN MADRID

Municipal Tourist Information Office
3 Plaza Mayor
☎ 91 366 54 77.

RENFE (Spanish Rail)
☎ 902 24 02 02 (24hrs).

British Airways
☎ 902 111 333
Mon.-Fri. 9am-7pm,
Sat. 9am-2pm.

Iberia
Information and reservations
☎ 902 400 500.

Madrid-Barajas Airport
☎ 91 305 86 56.

Health and safety emergencies (ambulances)
☎ 112

Serious ambulance emergencies
☎ 061

Police and Fire Brigade
Fire Brigade ☎ 080
Guardia Civil ☎ 062
Violence, theft, etc. ☎ 091
Municipal Police ☎ 092

Duty chemists ☎ 098

Lost property
Plaza de Legazpi, 7
☎ 91 588 43 46.

transport and entertainment. To give an idea of prices, a tapas meal with drinks costs around €12, dinner at a restaurant costs about €30, a single metro ticket costs €1.10 and a 10-ride bus and metro ticket costs €5.20, a short taxi ride costs €3, entry to a disco costs in the region of €18, a museum ticket costs €3 and a flamenco show with drinks costs around €30. Only taxi rides and drinks are really cheap.

HEALTH

No vaccinations are needed before entering the country. EU citizens should obtain form E111 from their local post offices before departure and will then be entitled to claim the cost of any medical assistance. You should be able to find most of the pharmaceutical products you are used to in Madrid,. However, if you're on a course of medical treatment, it's advisable to take enough medicine with you as you can never be sure of finding the exact one in Madrid.

LOCAL TIME

Spain is normally one hour ahead of Greenwich Mean Time except in summertime, from the end of March to the end of September, when clocks are put forward an hour, and the time difference is two hours.

FESTIVALS AND HOLIDAYS

1 January: New Year's Day (*año nuevo*)

6 January: Epiphany (*día de los Reyes*)

19 March: San Jose's Day

March-April: Maundy Thursday and Good Friday (*jueves y viernes Santo*)

March-April: Easter Sunday (*día de Pascua*)

1 May: Labour Day (*día del Trabajo*)

2 May: Madrid Autonomous Community Day (*Comunidad de Madrid*)

15 May: San Isidro's Day (patron saint of Madrid)

13 June: San Antonio's Day (festival of unmarried girls)

15 August: Feast of the Assumption (*Asunción*)

12 October: Hispanidad Day (*día de la Hispanidad*, commemorating the discovery of America)

1 November: All Saints' Day (*todos los Santos*)

6 December: Constitution Day (*día de la Constitución*)

8 December: Immaculate Conception (*Immaculada Concepción*)

25 December: Christmas Day (*Navidad*)

TAPAS, CUISINE IN MINIATURE

Tapas aren't just snacks served as an accompaniment to drinks, as is often supposed – they represent a whole way of life. *Ir de tapas* is more than a quick drink and a bite to eat, it means spending time in good company, with good conversation, over an aperitif and delighting in dishes of tasty specialities served on the counters of bars and taverns.

and the way they are prepared and served has changed. On Sundays and holidays popular haunts are filled with families and groups of friends enjoying these delicacies. If the popularity of tapas bars is anything to go by, this culinary art is far from having exhausted itself and still has plenty of surprises in store.

AN ANDALUSIAN LEGEND

Tapas are said to have originated in Andalusia and spread throughout the entire Iberian peninsular. According to tradition, the word *tapa* (cover) originally came from the barkeeper's practice of covering wine glasses with a piece of bread, or a slice of cheese or ham to keep out the flies. This later developed into the tradition of serving a plate of snacks as an accompaniment for wine and sherry.

A CHANGING TRADITION

Tapas now serve a very different purpose from their original Andalusian role. They are no longer seen simply as snacks and often replace traditional meals. Even their appearance

HOT TAPAS

There are literally dozens of different kinds of hot tapas for you to try, but the ones listed here are quite unmissable.
Gambas a la plancha: prawns fried or grilled with garlic.
Almejas or *Mejillones a la marinera*: clams or mussels cooked in a white wine sauce.
Chipirones en su tinta: squid cooked in ink.
Pimientos fritos de Padrón: small pieces of fried green pepper in salt.
Tortilla de patatas fritas: potato omelette.
Huevos revueltos: omelette and vegetables.
Revueleto de esparragos: omelette and asparagus.

COLD TAPAS

The more traditional varieties are also the best.

Jamón, lomo, morcilla, chorizo: portions of ham, cured meats, spicy sausage etc.

Queso manchego: cheese.

Patatas fritas a la inglesa: crisps.

Boquerones en vinagre: anchovies marinated in vinegar and garlic.

Pimientos del piquillo: red peppers marinated in olive oil.

Salpicón de mariscos: diced salad with seafood.

Cogollos: lettuce hearts with anchovies and olive oil.

SPECIALITIES OF THE MADRID *COMMUNIDAD*

Recipes vary from region to region, and even from bar to bar, but you can usually rely on the classics such as *tortilla*, which you'll find everywhere. While you're staying in the capital of tapas, take the opportunity of trying some of the local specialities:

Callos a la madrileña: tripe prepared the *Madrileño* way.

Albondigas en salsa: meat balls in tomato sauce.

Las croquetas: ham or chicken croquettes.

Las empañadillas de atún: tuna and tomato patties.

Las setas a la plancha: mushrooms with garlic.

WHERE TO TRY TAPAS

Posada de la Villa
Caja Baja, 9
☎ **91 366 18 80**
Mon.-Tue. 1-4pm, 8pm-midnight, Sun. 1-4pm.

You can try out the tapas at the counter of this bar and restaurant. The varieties on offer are traditional but they're particularly delicious here. It's an ideal place if you're trying them for the first time.

TORTILLA CON PATATAS FRITAS

Why not make your very own tapas? For six people, you will need:

5 large potatoes
2 onions
5 eggs
Salt and pepper.

Dice the potatoes and thinly slice the onions. Heat the olive oil in a frying pan, add the vegetables and fry until tender.

QUICK GUIDE TO ORDERING TAPAS

El pica-pica: appetisers (e.g. olives).

La tapa: a single serving, more substantial than a *pica-pica*.

Un montadito: a slice of white bread with anything in the way of a topping (an invitation to culinary inventiveness!), all held in place with a cocktail stick.

Bocadillos: sandwiches (can be filled with a portion of tapas)

Un canapé: a small open sandwich.

Un pincho: a portion (a slice of *tortilla*, a Dublin Bay prawn stuffed with anchovy, etc.

Una ración: a plate of tapas that serves two or three persons

Una pulga: a small finger roll with a variety of fillings.

Una caña: a small glass of beer.

Un tubo: a large glass of beer.

Season with salt and pepper. Beat the eggs, season and pour the mixture into the frying pan over the potatoes and onions. Fry gently for 5 or 6 minutes. Then turn the omelette over by sliding it on to a plate and gently turning it back into the pan to cook on the other side. *Tortilla con patatas fritas* is eaten cold and is quite delicious.

MADRID, CAPITAL OF THE *MARCHA*

To be *marchoso* is to spend the night partying, moving from one place to another. When Madrid emerged from the grip of Franco's regime, it adopted a love for life, culture and the arts. Its nightlife has become a never-ending display of bright lights and music and even if that's what you're looking for, you'll find it hard to keep track of all the sights and sounds of the city.

Francisco Franco.

THE *MOVIDA*

In the early 1980s, as the city emerged from the confines of Franco's authoritarian regime, it was gripped by a wave of creativity unparalleled in the rest of Europe. An influx of talented individuals from all over Spain coincided with the return of political refugees and the arrival of intellectuals from Latin America. A new generation, liberated from traditional values and ways of life, soon added spice to the cocktail. The *Movida* ('action') symbolised movement, freedom, celebration and creation. In the eyes of some of its founders, such as the cult film director Pedro Almodóvar, it's now no more than a distant memory. Judge for yourself.

HOW TO SPEND A NIGHT OUT IN MADRID

Bistros:
these are quiet places where you can talk and read in peace, both in the daytime and in the evening.

Tapas bars or *tascas*:
here you can drink wine or beer while enjoying a selection of tapas.

***Cervecerías*:**
these resemble tapas bars but generally have a wider choice of beers. One of the most famous is the *Cervecería Alemana* in Plaza Santa Ana.

The Pachá, a former theatre converted into a disco.

***Copas* bars:**
these open from 10pm to 3am and are more original. They each have culinary and musical specialities (see p. 120).

They sell beer or stronger alcoholic drinks and they're all part of a circuit, so you go from one to another without ever staying in one for very long.

Clubs and discos: these start to get busy at around 3am. Plentiful and varied, they were the spring-board of the *Movida* in the 1980s (see page 118).

Late bars: some clubs open at 5am and don't close until around 11am – and they're always packed. Before going to bed after a night on the town, it's tradition to go for *chocolate con churros* (hot chocolate with doughnuts).

TABLAOS FLAMENCOS AND *SALAS ROCIERAS*

Late every evening *tablaos* (flamenco clubs) stage performances by **flamenco** singers and dancers. While they're often rejected by

aficionados because of the number of foreign tourists eager for a taste of folklore who attend them, the clubs neverthess offer very high-quality entertainment.

The **salas rocieras** stage **rociero ballets**, to the music of **sevillanas** (a folk dance that strongly influenced flamenco). If you feel like it, there's nothing to stop you taking part in the festivities and dancing a *sevillana*. Do note that all the dances follow strict movements and none of the steps are improvised, so make sure you and your partner know the moves before you get on the dance floor!

FLAMENCO ARTISTS IN VOGUE

Cantaores **(singers)**: Miguel Poveda, from Barcelona (and not a gypsy), Fernando Terremoto, the son of a famous *cantaor* (Terremoto de Jérez, of gypsy origin), El Falo, a gypsy from Asturias, Maïté Martín, from Barcelona, and Estrella Morente, daughter of the celebrated Enrique Morente, as well as José Merced, Chano Lobato and Carmen Linares. *Bailaores* **(dancers)**: Eva Lahierbabuena, Sara Baras, Joaquín Cortes, Antonio Canales and Candelo el Grilo. **Guitarists**: Tomatito, Vicente Amigo and Paco de Lucia.

performances known as *fiestas de zarzuela* were staged. Penned by the great Spanish playwrights of the Golden Age (Lope de Vega and Calderón de la Barca), this musical theatre first put the emphasis on literary erudition. Later, the *zarzuela chico* became popular. The *zarzuela grande* adopted a form of comic opera, similar to French operetta, combining old-fashioned charm with the irresistible *joie de vivre* of Madrid. Until recently the lively tunes and melodies of the *zarzuela* only reached the ears of septuagenarians, but now audiences of all ages flock to the theatres.

MADRID BY NIGHT

If you've already succumbed to Madrid's charms, you'll find it takes on a very different appearance after nightfall. For a tour of its most beautiful sights, start in Plaza de Cánovas del Castillo, where you can admire the Fountain of Neptune before making

The Fountain of Neptune, Plaza de Cánovas del Castillo.

THE *ZARZUELA*

In Madrid at the turn of the 17th century, in a royal palace surrounded by bramble hedges (*zarzales*), magnificent theatrical and musical

your way down Calle Alcalá. At its intersection with Calle Gran Vía, note the magnificently illuminated buildings. When you get to Puerta del Sol, end your walk via Plaza Mayor.

PATISSERIE FROM HEAVEN

There's nothing quite like the patisserie of Madrid. Surprisingly enough, some of the finest specialities originated in convents and monasteries. It may not be to everyone's taste to eat a cake dedicated to a saint or named after a man of the cloth, but at least it's highly original. Like the people of Madrid, you too can succumb to an age-old tradition and indulge in a selection from one of the mouth-watering displays of cakes and pastries.

ROSCON DE REYES

Epiphany, on 6 January, marks an important day for children in Spain.

It's the day they receive their presents. Every family feels duty-bound to buy a *roscon de reyes*, a kind of orange or almond-flavoured brioche topped with candied fruit, to mark the occasion, though more so in the capital than elsewhere. The recipe for *roscon de reyes* has remained unchanged since its invention by the chefs of the first Bourbon kings.

PANECILLOS DEL SANTO

Another particularly good time to try Madrid patisserie is 17 January, San Antonio Abad's Day, the patron saint of animals. Anyone who owns an animal can take it to be blessed at the church of San Anton (Calle Hortaleza). Even if you haven't brought your faithful friend with you, you needn't miss out on the *panecillos del santo* sold by the local parish priest. These little round biscuits are decorated with a cross and it's said to be a good idea to buy an extra one, wrap it in foil and leave it with your money – that way, financial worries will be a thing of the past.

TORRIJAS AND MONAS DE PASCUA

Easter week is the traditional time when *torrijas* are served. A *torrija* is a bit like French toast, made by soaking a slice of bread in milk, cinnamon and sugar and then frying it. It tastes even more delicious with honey or sugar and cinnamon sprinkled on top. There's even a kind of *torrija* made by first soaking the bread in pale sherry. The Easter festivities are also the time when small, sweet brioches known as *monas de pascua* are eaten. These are round and flat and served with a hard-boiled egg in its shell on top. They're one curiosity that you really shouldn't miss.

ROSQUILLAS DEL SANTO

These small macaroons are eaten on 15 May, San Isidro's Day, the patron saint of Madrid. There are three kinds – *tonta* ('the idiot'), which is aniseed-flavoured and not very sweet, *lista* (the 'intelligent one'), which is iced and sweeter, and the *Santa Clara*. If you can't make up your mind between the *tonta* and the *lista*, do what many of the *Madrileños* do – buy both and take a bite of each in turn.

SUSPIROS DE MODISTILLAS

It's not all that long ago that the needle-women of Madrid would go to the very popular *verbena* (festival) near the church of San Antonio de la Florida on 13 June. It was said that if they threw a needle into the holy water without missing, they'd find a fiancé within the year. The *verbena* is still going strong, but the *suspiros de modistillas* ('needlewomen's sighs'), small meringues sandwiched together with praline, are even more popular.

HUESOS DE SANTOS, BUNUELOS DE VIENTO AND PANELLES

On All Saints' Day it's the custom to buy *huesos de santos*. These are delicious marzipan sweetmeats made in the form of cannelloni stuffed with praline, coconut or one of many other fillings. If you don't like marzipan, you can always opt to try the *bunuelos de viento*, which are small cream or praline-flavoured puffs. The *panelles*, small balls of *mazapan* (marzipan) decorated with pine nuts, originated in Catalonia.

CORONA DE ALMUDENA

These cream or chocolate-filled brioches are sold on 8 November, St Almudena's Day. *Corona de Almudena* are less fashionable than they once were, but they're just as delicious as ever.

MAZAPANES, POLVORONES, MANTECADOS AND TURRÓN

Christmas is one of the most important times of year for confectioners. Many sweet specialities with a strongly oriental flavour make their appearance, their origins dating back to the Arab conquest of Spain in AD 711. *Mazapan* takes the form of figurines. *Polvorones* are made from powdered almonds, cinnamon, sesame and sugar. A derivative of these little biscuits, *mantecados*, can also be found. The recipe is the same except for the addition of white wine. The handmade *turrón*, (nougat) which bears little resemblance to its industrially-made counterpart, takes on some very unusual flavours, including pineapple, orange, pistachio, walnut, rum and raisin, and coconut.

CHURROS

One morning, instead of having breakfast at your hotel, follow the *Madrileño* custom of going to a local bistro and ordering *cafe con churros*. These long, ridged doughnuts can also be found in *churrerías*.

ANGUILAS DE MAZAPAN

It's difficult to say whether *anguilas de mazapan* is a pastry or a work of art. Sold at Christmas time, this crown-shaped mixture of brioche and marzipan, decorated with candied fruit and carved meringue figures is something you really shouldn't miss. From cherubs to dragons to the Victory of Samothrace to Venus de Milo, craftsmen give free rein to their talents.

FESTIVALS AND TRADITIONS

The Madrid year is littered with traditional festivals both religious and secular. The Spanish love to gather in the streets to watch the procession of the Three Kings, admire the fantastic costumes at carnival time, attend the popular *verbenas* and follow the colourful processions of Easter week.

THE CHRISTMAS FESTIVITIES

This particular time of year sees the people of Madrid flocking in droves to the Plaza Mayor for the traditional Christmas market. The skilfully-arranged figures of the Nativity scene are the star attraction. On the Saturday before 24 December, a singing competition on the theme of the Nativity, the popular *Certamen de Villancicos*, is held in the Centro Cultural de la Villa in Plaza Colon. The children of Madrid have to wait patiently until 5 January, the day before Epiphany, for their presents. This is when the procession of the Wise Men accompanied by their followers takes place. Leaving the Parque del Retiro at around 4pm, they parade slowly, arriving in Plaza Mayor at around 8pm, where they perform a ritual of asking the children if they've been good. It's only after they get home that the youngsters find their gifts waiting for them.

THE PREGÓN

Whether it's for San Isidro's Day, Christmas, Easter or the carnival, the start of the festivities is always announced by the *pregón*. This is a famous artist or sports personality who is specially recruited for the purpose by the town hall of Madrid. A ceremony takes place in the Plaza Mayor or Plaza de la Villa. Many of Madrid's inhabitants come to hear the *pregón's* speech and listen to the music that follows it.

THE CARNIVAL

Long prohibited under the Franco regime, the carnival celebrations are a magnificent spectacle. Leaving Calle Bailén, the floats make their way to Plaza Mayor. Here both adults and children can take part in a fancy-dress competition. Many evening events are staged in Madrid.

Don't miss the one held at the Real Academia de Bellas Artes, a fabulous party where much of the building is given over to numerous orchestras. If you can't afford the entry fee (around €36), just wait around outside as the arrival of the procession alone is a sight worth seeing.

EASTER WEEK

On Maundy Thursday and Good Friday, the streets of Madrid teem with processions held in honour of Jesus or the Virgin Mary. The Virgin's statue is decked out in all its finery, and laden with flowers and jewels.

SAN ISIDRO'S DAY

San Isidro is the patron saint of Madrid. After the opening of the festivities by the *pregón* in Plaza Mayor, the whole city comes to life, with exhibitions, competitions and celebrations.

The period around 15 May, which marks the start of the *mundial de toros*, is of the greatest importance for aficionados of bullfighting. But the most popular festival of all is undoubtedly the *Romería* (or *Verbena*) in the Parque de San Isidro, which takes place right opposite the Ermita de San Isidro in the very popular Carabanchel district. During a *verbena*, many *Madrileños* come dressed as *chulapos* and *chulapas* (the traditional costume of Madrid, *chulo* meaning elegant) and loaded down with picnics to enjoy the programme of music, tombolas, barbecues, *chorizo*, *churros* and a variety of competitions and events.

OTHER VERBENAS

On 13 June a very popular *verbena* takes place next to the Ermita de San Antonio de la Florida (Paseo de la Florida, 5), with music, dancing, *churros* and barbecues. On 15 August, you can also watch the procession of the Virgen de la Paloma, to the church of La Paloma in Puerta de Toledo. The

procession is followed by another *verbena*, this time in the Las Vistillas district.

THE *CASTIZO*

Dressed in his *parpusa* (black and white checked hat), *safo* (white scarf) and black and white three-piece suit, the *castizo* parades on the arm of his female counterpart, the *castiza*, who wears a white percale blouse, black skirt and the well-known embroidered shawl known as *mantones de Manilla*. The term *castizo* refers to the culture of the traditional working classes of Madrid and they seize every opportunity to remind people of their folklore, which also is reflected in the famous *Madrileño* dance, the *chotis*.

Church of La Paloma.

BULLFIGHTING AND BEYOND

Bullfighting is part of the cultural heritage of the Iberian peninsular. On horseback or foot, it's a source of pride for the Spanish, whether they're fans or not. A *corrida* at Las Ventas de Madrid is still an authentic and prestigious display.

LAS VENTAS, THE MECCA OF BULLFIGHTING
Calle Alcalá, 237
☎ 91 356 22 00.

Las Ventas is considered to be the foremost bullring in the world, although it can actually accommodate fewer spectators than those in Mexico. It's a beautiful building, with arched galleries and decorative tiling. Inside the Spanish-Moorish portals, people from all walks of life witness the excitement of the bullfight. The atmosphere is a strange mixture of tension, joy, shared experience, discord and plain hostility.

THE *FERIA* OF SAN ISIDRO

For nearly 50 years, the *feria* of San Isidro (the patron saint of the city) has been a cultural and social phenomenon. Between 15 May and early June the bullfighting event of the year takes place. Aficionados from all over the world gather to witness the *corridas* and discuss the history of bullfighting and all the latest news. The greatest matadors have paraded here, including Litri, El Cordobes, Espartaco and Cesar Rincón. Lectures, exhibitions, films and tributes all feature on the agenda.

HOW TO GET TICKETS FOR BULLFIGHTS

You can buy tickets in Plaza de Las Ventas or from Localidades Galicia (Plaza del Carmen, 1, ☎ 91 531 27 32). It's even possible to get seats at the very last moment. Large numbers of ticket touts hang about outside the bullring before every *corrida*, but the prices they demand are exorbitant. If you're out of luck, you can still catch a glimpse of the bulls. The day before each *corrida*, they can be seen in La Venta del Batan in Casa del Campo.

THE HAUNTS OF THE AFICIONADOS

The Hotel Wellington, a few hundred metres/yards from Las Ventas, belongs to the Baltasar Iban family of bull breeders. The *mundillo* (world) of bullfighting congregates here. Impressarios, breeders and middlemen of every kind, discuss and fix the prices, agree exclusive contracts and put together the programme for the season. The *toreros* dress at the Hotel Reina Victoria and some frequent the *De Torres* bar (Calle Alcalá, 235) for a coffee before the start of the bullfight. After the *corrida*, the celebrations continue in the bars around Plaza Monumental or in the small restaurants *con ambiente torino*. Don't be put off by the tacky appearance of the Café Sierra (Calle Villa Franca,

11). The food is delicious and the owner is passionate about bulls and bullfighting. At *Donde Leo* (Calle Pedro Heredia, 22) you can try oxtail specialities. The owner, a *cantaor* (flamenco singer), sings after the meal and, at midnight, everyone strikes ups the famous song *Salve Rociera*. There's never a lack of atmosphere.

QUICK GUIDE TO BULLFIGHTING

Torero: fights 4-year-old bulls.
Novillero: fights 3-year-old bulls.
Alternative: the ceremony in which a *novillero*, accompanied by a sponsor, becomes a *torero*.
Faena: the moment before the kill when the *torero*, alone with his adversary, makes passes with the *muleta*, a red cloth stretched on a stick.
Estocade: the *torero* sticks his sword between the bull's

TWO WOMEN IN A MAN'S WORLD

Born in Madrid in 1972, Cristina Sanchez has written a new page in the history of bullfighting. She was the first woman to pass the *alternative*, at Nîmes in 1996 and has since managed to win over the Madrid audience, which is reputed to be very demanding and chauvinistic. In 1997, Maripaz Vega, another female figure in the male-dominated world of bullfighting, became the only woman to have passed the *alternative* in Spain.

THE 'MOZART' OF BULLFIGHTING

A new idol of the bullring, Julian Lopez, known as El Juli, was born in Madrid in 1982. He fought his first calf at the age of eight and began bullfighting in earnest in Mexico in 1997. Since then, he's become a smash hit. His genius lies in resurrecting old passes and inventing new ones. In September 1998 in Las Ventas, while he was still a *novillero*, he won the hearts and admiration of enthusiasts by fighting six bulls in a row. The bullring was full that day, which is a rare occurrence. He passed the *alternative* a few days later.

SPANISH WINE

Spain is one of the world's largest wine-producing countries, best known for quality reds from Rioja and sherry from Jerez. There are a wealth of excellent Spanish wines and a stay in Madrid could be an opportunity to taste some unfamiliar ones that are worth getting to know, such as *Priorato* and *Ribera del Duero*.

RIOJA

With 36,150 hectares/89,320 acres of vineyards and an average annual production of 176,500,000 litres, Rioja is one of the oldest and most prolific wine-producing regions in Spain. During the 19th century, when an outbreak of phylloxera ruined most of the grape harvest in the Bordeaux region, wine merchants turned to the Rioja producers to buy their wine. By exporting French know-how, these merchants contributed to the improvement of Spanish wine-making methods, especially in the use of oak casks. The Baron de Chirel wine, founded in 1860 is a blend of cabernet-sauvignon and *tempranillo* (the most highly regarded Spanish vine), and is probably one of the oldest and best wines produced in Spain.

VEGA SICILIA, A LEGENDARY WINE

This wine is without a doubt not only the most prestigious in Spain but also amongst the best-known in the world. It's very difficult to find a bottle to buy, but you can taste it in some of the larger restaurants. Its price is matched only by its quality and rarity. Made in the Ribera del Duero region, just north of Madrid, it's a skilful blend of Cabernet Sauvignon, Tempranillo, Malbec and Merlot grapes. Just thirty years ago, *Vega Sicilia* was the only wine produced in the area. Its prestige led to the emergence of new wines, such as *Pesquera*, *Val Sotillo* and *Abadia Retuerta*. Today, with 12,500 hectares/30,900 acres of vineyards and an average annual production of 17,000,000 litres of wine, Ribera del Duero has become Spain's most fashionable red wine-producing region and is vying with Rioja for first place. You can take this opportunity to make your own decision.

NEW VARIETIES AND LABELS

Over the past few years, the price of the more prestigious Iberian wines has increased considerably. This has led the Spanish wine growers to try new grape varieties that are less well-known but also less expensive. Priorato (which originated in Catalonia) is benefiting most from this new trend. Among the wines whose standing is improving you'll find the Somontano label, as well as Bodega Pirineos, a blend of cabernet-sauvignon and merlot grapes, (expect to pay around €6 for a bottle of the 1997 *reserva*) and Navarra, a combination of Tempranillo and Cabernet Sauvignon (the *Nekeas* 1996 *reserva* costs in the region of €54 a bottle).

GOOD WINES AT REASONABLE PRICES

The relatively high price of the great French wines is one reason why Spanish wines have increasingly made their mark. Among the more memorable of these are the Atardi Grandes Anadas 94, a Rioja that was awarded an amazing 96 out of a possible 100 points by one of the world's leading wine experts, Robert Parker. As you may imagine, its price has risen accordingly (€96 a bottle). But don't worry, there are other good Spanish wines still to be had at perfectly affordable prices. Here are some that are worth a try.

Ribera del Duero:
Teofilo Reyes, 1996 *reserva*, around €14.

Rioja:
Vina Dorada, 1994 *reserva*, around €12
Vina Ardanza, 1990 *reserva*, around €14.

Priorato:
Martinet Bru, 1996 *reserva*, around €9.

THE WHITE WINES OF GALICIA

Galicia, in the north-west of the country is the home of white wine. A rugged, wet region, it produces several local varieties of grape, Albarino and Godello being the most widespread. But the best vine is probably the Lurton. It takes its name from its owner, Brigitte Lurton, who comes from a family of wine producers from the Bordelais region of France. A 1997 *reserva* sells for the handsome sum of around €20 a bottle, which suggests there's good drinking in store.

JEREZ

You may not have realised it, but there are many types of sherry. They range from *secos,* that are drunk as an aperitif,

to *dulces* that are served to accompany desserts. Among the latter, there are various categories to suit all tastes, including *finos, manzanillas, amontillado* (very dry) and *oloroso* (the sweetest). Not to everyone's taste, sherry is usually served in Spain with accompanying dishes of olives, almonds or grilled specialities. Do try *mojama* (a sort of dried tuna) with an *oloroso* – it's a marriage made in heaven.

CAVA

While a wide variety of wines are produced in Spain, the same can't be said of sparkling wines. Comparitively little of it is produced and it's therefore quite expensive. However, *Cava*, perhaps not as fine as champagne, has proved a popular export. For wine buffs, small family producers, such as Agusi Torello and Recaredo, are recommended. They're just as good as the giants Codorniu and Frexeneit.

SPANISH PAINTING AND THE GOLDEN AGE

El Greco, Velázquez and Goya stand out as the great names of classical Spanish painting. The 17th century heralded the start of the Golden Age of Spanish art and literature. The Seville School, to which Zurbarán, Murillo and Velázquez belonged, played a prominent role in the period. The paintings of the time tended to have religious themes, showing the strong sway of the Catholic church; depictions of landscapes and still lifes were rare. Between the 16th century, with its Italian influence, and the 18th century, with its French influence, the Golden Age saw the appearance of many great artists.

Murillo: San Diego de Alcalá Feeding the Poor.

Murillo.

A HISTORICALLY DECADENT CENTURY

With no worthy successor to Emperor Charles V (Carlos I of Spain) or Felipe II, Spain gradually began to lose its influence in 17th-century Europe. The weakness of the ruling house of Habsburg signalled the twilight of the dynasty, and the country entered a period of decline. Catalonia rebelled, Portugal and the Netherlands seized their independence and Spain

exhausted itself in a series of ruinous wars that marked the end of its power in Europe. Struck down by epidemics and famine, the population deserted the land, leaving it in the hands of the Church and the aristocracy. Against this backdrop of economic deterioration an extraordinary artistic flowering took place, a period known as the Golden Age.

ART IN CONTEXT

In the 16th century, Spanish painting was marked by a decrease in Flemish influence. The spirit of the Renaissance had spread from its native Italy throughout Europe. El Greco was the great master of the century. The first half of the 17th century was dominated by a style of realism inspired by the Italians. Subjects such as

One of the Goya rooms in the Museo del Prado.

mysticism, contemplative works and scenes of Christian martyrdom exalted the principles of the Counter Reformation. The influence of artists such as Caravaggio, can be seen in the play of light and emerging realism. Velázquez was one of the heirs of this tradition. The second half of the 17th century was influenced by the Flemish painter Rubens, who used dynamic compositions and light colours. Along with theatrical Baroque design, it was the start of a period of brilliance and inspiration. The 18th century saw the rise to power of the Bourbons, marking the onset of artistic impoverishment compared with the richness of the Golden Age. Nevertheless, it gave birth to one of the country's great geniuses, Francisco de Goya.

Domingo el Antiguo. Settling permanently in the Spanish city, he became a great success and lead a sumptuous, worldly life away from the court, counting among his friends some of the great men of the century – Cervantes, Lope de Vega and Góngora. Though influenced by the Italian Renaissance, he gradually abandoned its sensuous forms to evolve a personal style of bright colours painted in an intense religious fervour that expressed itself dramatically on the canvas. You can see the *Baptism of Christ*, one of his major works, in the Prado.

VELÁZQUEZ

Born in Seville, Velázquez played a unique role in Spanish art, in terms of both technique and visualisation. Having painted a successful portrait of King Felipe IV in 1623, he settled in Madrid. The Court facilitated his access to the best schools and he twice visited Italy. He returned from these journeys with heightened sensitivity, a finer stroke and a more subtle perception of light and colour. Among his countless paintings, the *Gardens of the Villa Medici*, in the Prado, expresses this Italian influence.

El Greco: La Sagrada Familia.

EL GRECO

Born in Crete in 1541, El Greco ('the Greek') spent his childhood in Greece before moving to Venice, where Titian was master. In 1570 he went to Rome where he discovered Mannerism (the introduction of sentiment into art). In 1577 he left Italy and came to Toledo to paint the altarpiece in the convent of Santo

Velázquez: La Fragua de Vulcano.

MONARCHY AND A POPULAR KING

There's no getting away from it, King Juan Carlos and his family are universally popular and respected by the Spanish people. Despite his troubled past, the King of Spain has succeeded in establishing himself by peaceful means and by making a real effort to adapt to the realities of modern, and above all European, life. Don't expect to find gossip or photos of the royal family in the popular press, they avoid the escapades of some other royal families.

BOURBONS ON THE THRONE OF SPAIN

Without going into the history of Spain in detail, it may be useful to know a few facts. In 1700 Carlos II, the last of the Habsburg line, died without issue having chosen Felipe V, Duke of Anjou and grandson of the French king Louis XIV and the infanta Maria Teresa, to succeed him. In the reign of Carlos III, Madrid started to develop into a modern city. The 19th century opened to the War of Independence, fought against the troops of Napoleon. The Carlist Wars succeeded them, fought by the supporters of Isabel II and the supporters of Don Carlos, the queen's uncle. The first Republic lasted only a year, after which Spain

went into politcal decline, remaining neutral during World War I. Surviving two dictatorships, the advent of the Republic and a civil war that nearly destroyed the country, Spain now lives under a monarchy, with Juan Carlos at its head.

Carlos III.

THE COMING TO POWER OF JUAN CARLOS

After years of dictatorship by Primo de Rivera and later Franco, the General named Juan Carlos as his successor in 1969, six years before his death. Spanish legislation is carried out by the *Cortes* (parliament) and supervised by the National Council. As Head of State and Head of the Armed Forces, the king gives his assent to the composition of the government, in which he plays an important part.

EL 23 F (PRONOUNCED EFE)

On 23 February 1981 soldiers, led by Civil Guard colonel Antonio Tejero burst into the Spanish parliament, confined the deputies and seized the television studios. The Spanish people followed the attempted coup d'etat throughout the night on television. As Head of the Armed Forces, King Juan Carlos refused to support the rebels and demanded they surrender, thus saving Spanish democracy. The king's image emerged much strengthened from this test.

A UNITED FAMILY

Juan Carlos married Sofia of Greece in 1962 and they have three children, the infantas Elena and Cristina, and Prince Felipe. The infantas are both married and no longer live at home, but the family likes to meet up for the holidays. It's a chance for them to appear smiling and united in the press. Sofia is known for her intelligence and devotion to her role as First Lady of Spain. While remaining outside the political arena, she plays an important social role and has encouraged a large number of cultural initiatives.

On the death of the dictator, Franco, the king showed great courage, an iron will and a strong sense of diplomacy in supporting the Prime Minister, Adolfo Suárez, in his task of liberalisation and creating a new democracy. Smiling, friendly and relaxed, the king showed himself to be a true leader. An aficionado of bullfighting and a motorbike enthusiast, he is supportive towards his own family and very close to his subjects. During official ceremonies, he never hesitates to break with the usual protocol and shake the outstretched hands of his admiring public.

THE HEIR TO THE THRONE

Felipe, Prince of Asturias, was born in 1968. He was a student at a public university in Madrid before completing his studies at the University of Georgetown in the United States. He already represents his father on journeys abroad. Informal, and seen as easily accessible, he has presented a Spanish nature programme on television. He is a bachelor and has only had a few *novias* (girlfriends). However, the press is vigilant, always on the lookout for a good match.

LAS INFANTES

Elena, Los Condes de Lugo, the eldest daughter of King Juan Carlos is married to Jaime de Marichalar. They have a son, Juan

Felipe and a daughter, Victoria. Elena plays a purely social role and lives in Madrid. Cristina, Los Condes de Palma, born in 1965, is married to Iñaki Undangarin, a professional handball player of Basque origin. The couple live in Barcelona and have three sons, Juan, Pablo and Miguel. Iñaki was selected for the Spanish handball team at the 2000 Olympic Games in Sydney, where his team won a bronze medal. Cristina is in charge of the programme for International Cooperation at the Fundación Caixa, the cultural foundation of the Catalan bank.

GAMBLING FEVER

T here are few *Madrileños* who don't try their luck at games of chance. Their *ilusión*, as a Castillian would call it, the wild dream of making a fortune, is kept alive by the lottery. Their fantasies of riches are a stark contrast to the blind ticket sellers who stand on street corners plying their trade. Who knows, maybe luck will smile on them next time.

MESMERISING FIGURES

The Spanish spend an alarming €1,500 (around £1,000) per person a year on Las Loterías y Apuestas del Estado – the multitude of lotteries and draws that are approved by the state – and the figure is continually increasing. By comparison, the average amount of £3.34 spent per person on each UK National Lottery draw seems quite reasonable!

THE PUBLIC SECTOR AND TRADITIONAL FORMS OF GAMBLING

When they want to try their luck, the Spanish have recourse to many traditional forms of gambling. The Loteria Nacional, which was started in 1812, is based on a random selection of numbers. The draws take place on Thursdays and Saturdays when the people of Madrid hope to at least double their initial outlay of €3, and dream of winning a great deal more.

Las Loterias y Apuestas del Estado records the highest number of participants, along with the special draws of the Loteria del Niño. The Loteria Primitiva which was started in 1763 in the reign of Carlos III, was suppressed in 1862 and finally re-established in 1985. A bit like bingo, you can, for example, win €5.50 with a €0.60 bet if you have three winning numbers. The Bono Loto is similar but even more affordable. You can place bets of €0.30 or more. For the more affluent, the Gordo Primitiva allows bigger wins with a minimum bet of €1.50. Lastly, the Quiniela de Futbol, which was set up in 1946, is the equivalent of British football pools. You have to predict the results of the 15 football matches shown on the ticket. Surprisingly enough for a country of football fanatics, this particular form of gambling hasn't been a great success.

THE LOTERIA DE NAVIDAD, A MADRID INSTITUTION

The Loteria de Navidad is a special draw that takes place on 23 December and the vast majority of Spaniards take part in it. It's so popular that if anyone forgets to buy a ticket, a friend or colleague will offer to sell them *un decimo* (a tenth) of their own. The tickets go on sale three months before the draw and every seller makes a point of displaying the winning tickets he has sold in the past. If you're listening to the radio on the day of the draw, don't be surprised if you hear a kind of litany – it's the announcement of the winning numbers. It's traditional for the winners of the Loteria de Navidad to bet the same numbers on the Loteria del Niño. This second draw takes place on 5 January. If you're in Madrid over the Christmas period, why not join in the gambling fever and buy a ticket. On the evening of the draw, find a comfortable seat in a café with a television and take part in the collective hysteria.

THE SUCCESS OF THE PRIVATE SECTOR

While the Spanish don't hesitate to spend their money on the various state lotteries, the private sector nevertheless has the most success – thanks to the 222,767 bingo halls, slot machine arcades and casinos distributed throughout Spain, 29,600 of which are in Madrid. The amount spent on gambling of this type is estimated to be £2,500 per person a year.

THE ONCE

The aim of the ONCE (Organisacion Nacional de Ciergos Españoles), which was set up over sixty years ago, is to help the blind and severely visually impaired to take part in everyday life. The organisation currently has over 50,000 employees. Its amazing success rests on the sale of lottery tickets in the street which provides the blind and visually impaired with stable employment. The money raised has been used to set up social services, such as the training of guide dogs, the special education of children and adults and the creation of a museum for the blind and visually impaired.

CHARCUTERIE AND CHEESE

Los embutidos (charcuterie) and cheese have always had a special importance in Spain, especially during times of hardship. With the food processing industry ensuring hygienic production, charcuterie and cheese have become not just staple foods but gourmet products that you really cannot afford to miss.

SERRANO OR *JÁBUGO*?

El jamón is simply the raw, cured, aged, unboned trotter or haunch of a pig. It comes with a variety of names – *Serrano*, *Ibérico*, *Pata negra*, *Bellota* and *Jábugo*. Which one should you choose? Some hams cost twice as much as others, so it's important to distinguish between them. *Cerdo ibérico* pigs differs from other breeds in having black trotters, hence their nickname *Pata Negra* (black feet). Fed mainly on acorns, they live in areas rich in oak trees (Salamanca, Cáceres, Badajoz, Córdoba, Seville, Málaga, Cádiz and Huelva). In order for the ham to be designated a true *jamón de*

Bellota, the pig must be fed exclusively on acorns, otherwise it's *jamón de recebo* (fed on animal feed). In each case, the hams are aged for at least two years. The best ham is *jamón de Bellota*, whatever its region of origin, with the prize for the tastiest ham going to *Jábugo* (from the Huelva region), which is cured in the cold, dry mountain air of Andalusia, and *Guijuelo* (from the Salamanca region), whose flavour and texture are quite superb. *Jamón de Serrano,* is also a raw, cured ham, but one that has been aged for less than two years. It may be less mature than the other hams, but it's still an excellent ham at a very affordable price.

CURED HAM, KING OF CHARCUTERIE

Ham, salt-cured, dried in mountain (*serrano*) air and aged for only a short time, has been around since Roman times, when it was eaten as an appetiser at the start of meals or as a snack to accompany drinks. Although the French claim to have invented it, it actually originated in Spain.

HOW TO SERVE *JAMÓN*

Whether it's *Serrano* or *de Bellota*, a *jamón* must be served in the correct way. Very thin slices 3-4cm/1-1¹/₂in wide are cut from the joint using a long, flexible, extremely sharp knife. The finer the slices, the better the ham. It must be kept at room temperature, not in a refrigerator. The dry part is discarded.

MORCILLA

Popular for over five hundred years in Spanish cuisine, the *morcilla* is a kind of spicy black pudding. A length of intestine is filled with a mixture of blood, spices and a variety of other ingredients, then cooked to form a black sausage. The ingredients vary according to the region and can include rice, onions, pine nuts and different spices, such as cinnamon. Cut into thick slices and fried, it's quite often served by the *ración* or *demi-ración* as an aperitif.

EL PATE LACÓN

Pate lacón is a partly-cooked pig's trotter, eaten finely sliced, just like *Ibérico* ham. It's absolutely delicious, so give it a try.

EL CHORIZO

The best part of the pig for making *chorizo* is traditionally the back. Once it's been aged and smoked, the raw meat is mixed with chilli and formed into a small sausage. Depending on how long it's been matured, it will be labelled *curado* or *semi-curado*. Originating from Estremadura, it's now produced in other parts of Spain, including Cantimpalos (Segovia), La Rioja and Pamplona. Mass production processes have caused it to lose some of its prestige, but served fried or raw, in sandwiches or as a *ración*, it's a staple of Spanish cuisine. If you take some home with you, go for *chorizo semi-curado*, which keeps better.

QUESO MANCHEGO, SPAIN'S GREATEST CHEESE

There's a limited choice of Spanish cheeses, but *queso*

WHERE TO BUY YOUR CHEESE AND HAM

El Palacio de los Quesos Calle Mayor, 53
☎ 91 548 16 23
Mon.-Fri. 9am-2.30pm, 5-8.30pm, Sat. 9am-2.30pm.

If, after tasting a particular cheese, you want to bring some back, this little shop offers a choice of over 80 cheeses, most of which are from Spain. They'll be happy to advise you on which will travel well. You'll also find a wide choice of charcuterie and cheese at **Corte Inglés** (see p. 109).

manchego is well worth trying. It's a favourite *ración* of *Madrileños* at tapas time. The different varieties – *manchego de oveja* (goat's milk) and *de vaca* (cow's milk), *curado*, *semi-curado*, *seco* and *blando* etc. – all come from the Castilla La Mancha area and vary in taste and texture depending upon their maturity, from fully mature (*añejo*), which is hard like parmesan, to the mild, softer *semi-curado* and the sharper *curado*.

FÚTBOL, KING OF SPORTS

Fútbol is played all over the world, and Spain is no exception to the rule. Everyone takes a keen interest in the sport. Differences of generation and sex vanish in the face of an all-consuming passion shared by one and all. This is easy to comprehend when you realise that the two Madrid clubs are among the best in Europe. Their exploits are closely followed and the players are international stars who are idolised.

A BIG DEAL

Fútbol has managed to enlist the support of thousands of Madrid's inhabitants by means of large, active associations of *socios* (subscribing members). Its audience has even at times given it a political dimension. Franco was the first to use Real Madrid's excellent results for propaganda purposes, however this was turned against him when the silent majority used the banners of Barcelona football club to express local nationalist feelings when Catalan flags were banned by the dictator. This proves that football is no longer simply a sport.

FOOTBALL, FOOTBALL EVERYWHERE

Every Sunday in the stadium, in bistros, at home in front of the television or glued to the radio, the Spanish think of nothing but football. Life simply stops for 90 minutes. The commentators are hysterical and the newspapers speculate on the results well in advance. The players arouse the passions of the supporters and are praised to the skies one day and cursed the next. It would be a mistake to miss out on the sport. The football stadiums are as much a part of Madrid as Las Ventas or the Prado.

REAL MADRID OR ATLETICO?

As a matter of principle, but all in good spirit, but no-one is neutral here. You have to choose which side you're on. Two major clubs confront one another in the capital, Real and Atletico. Real is considered an elite club. World-renowned, it boasts the finest collection of trophies in Europe. Great players, such as Kopa, Puskas, Di Stephano and Brutagueño, as well as Hierro, Raúl, Ronaldo, Zidane and Roberto Carlos, have all played for the club. Its stadium, Santiago

Bernabeu lies in the north of the city, along the Castellana. It's frequented by more supporters than any Plaza de Toros could accommodate and was the setting of the 1982 World Cup Final between Italy and Germany. Atletico unites the old working-class districts of the city. It's a different kind of club with more modest aspirations, cheaper tickets and, its supporters believe, a better atmosphere. Its red and white striped shirt is sure to feature in the championship of Spain (the *Liga*), even though it pulls off its finest victories in the Cup (the *Copa del Rey*). Its stadium, Vicente Calderon, is in the south of the city, on the banks of the Manzanares.

THE DERBY

Every year, the Atletico–Real derby arouses the fervent passions of both clubs' supporters and mobilises the whole of Madrid. This competition goes way beyond the context of a simple football match. The teams have to pull out all the stops for the honour of their individual camps. In the overexcited stadium, it can be a marvellous or a pitiful sight, depending upon whose side you are on!

FC BARCELONA, THE TRUE RIVAL OF THE *MADRILEÑOS*

Real Madrid's true rival is FC Barcelona. The battle between the two clubs is said to have started in 1943, during the semi-finals of the Spanish Cup. In the first leg Barcelona won 3-0 after a difficult game. The outcome seemed certain and some Madrid journalists even resorted to denouncing the behaviour of the Catalan supporters. In the return match, in front of hostile crowds, Real Madrid inflicted a humiliating 11-1 defeat on an intimidated FC Barcelona and qualified for the final.

Now, when the blue-and-red-clad players (Azulgranas) tread the Madrid turf in front of over 100,000 spectators, the atmosphere is electric and the whole of Catalonia turns out for the occasion. For the two football greats, who each year share the accolades, victory is an end in itself. Rivalry is so great that players opting to transfer from one team to another are said to have received death threats. The political circumstances of the country have given football a new dimension. The sport embodies the rivalry of Spain's two wealthiest regions. With every goal, Franco's scapegoat, Catalonia, earns the right to remind all comers that it exists, along with its culture and language. On the pitch, a whole region expresses its refusal to be assimilated in the kingdom and, in its own way, defies central government.

What to see Practicalities

GETTING AROUND MADRID

If you enjoy walking or taking a stroll, you can easily visit most of the centre of Madrid on foot. However, to get from one district to another, it's better to go by taxi. There are plenty of them about, they're very cheap and they don't mind taking you on short journeys. Hiring a car or using your own isn't really a good idea because it's difficult, not to say impossible, to drive and park in the narrow streets of Old Madrid.

THE METRO

The metro, or underground railway, consists of a network of 12 lines running every day from 6am to 1.30am. It's by far the fastest and easiest way of getting around the city. You can buy a single-journey ticket (€1.10 for an unlimited distance) or a metrobus ticket valid for 10 journeys by metro or bus (€5.20). These can be purchased at underground ticket offices.

For more information, contact: ☎ 91 468 42 00.

Two lines in particular will be very useful to you:

Line 5 (Canillejas-Aluche) serves the Rubén Darío, Alonso Martínez, Chueca, La Latina and Puerta de Toledo districts.

Line 2 (Ventas-Cuatro Caminos) will take you to the Parque del Retiro (get off at Retiro), the Prado museum (get off at Banco de España) and the Palacio Real (royal palace) (get off at Opera).

BUSES

These are very slow because of the sheer weight of the traffic in Madrid, but are still useful on the main roads (Paseo de la Castellana, Prado and Recoletos). They all have air conditioning and can be quite pleasant in summer. They run all day from 6am to midnight and some run all night as well (ask at tourist information offices).

SCOOTERS

It is possible to hire a scooter, but you need to be very careful as the traffic can be dangerous, especially in the city centre.

Motocicletas Antonio Castro
Calle Conde Duque, 13
☎ 91 542 06 57
Mon.-Fri. 9am-1pm,
4-7.30pm.

TAXIS

Taxis are without a doubt the most convenient and efficient way to travel about the city, especially since the fares are very reasonable. The good news is that there are over 15,000 taxis in Madrid. The official ones are white with a red trim and vacant taxis are easy to spot as they have green 'free' signs on their windscreens and green lights on their roofs. When they've finished work for the day, the drivers display their destinations in red.

You'll pay a supplement at night, on Sundays and holidays, at taxi ranks in stations and airports and at arenas and football stadiums. Whatever you do, don't forget to check that the driver starts the meter running.

Radio taxi
☎ 91 447 51 80

Tele taxi
☎ 91 371 21 31

Radioteléfono taxi
☎ 91 547 82 00 or
☎ 91 547 85 00

A BIRD'S-EYE VIEW OF THE CITY

For a really spectacular view, you can fly over Madrid in a helicopter. An hour's flight costs around €990 for a maximum of 5 people.

Aerodromo de Cuatro Vientos
Avenida del Valle, 13
☎ 91 553 85 01

SENDING POSTCARDS

You can buy stamps at post offices and tobacconists.

Palacio de Comunicaciones
(Main Post Office)
Plaza de Cibeles
Metro: Banco de España
☎ 902 197 197
Open Mon.-Fri.
8am-10pm,
Sat. 8.30am-2pm.

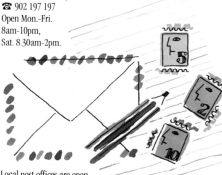

Local post offices are open from 8.30am to 8.30pm, sometimes with a break for lunch. It costs €0.50 to send a postcard or letter weighing up to 20gm to Europe, and €0.57 to the rest of the world. Letterboxes (mailboxes) are easy to spot – they're large with yellow lettering and are found at crossroads. The larger hotels also have a postal service.

TELEPHONING

The telephone boxes in Madrid take coins (50, 20, 10 and 5 cents) or cards (€10 or €5), which can be bought at tobacconists (*tabacs*), newspaper kiosks and post offices. Although cards offer no saving on calls – they're more convenient.

For information about Spain while you're there, call ☎ 1003

To phone Madrid from the UK, dial 00 34 followed by the 9 digits of the number you're calling. The dialling code for Madrid is 91. To telephone the UK from Madrid, dial 07 44 followed by the number you want minus the zero.

To call Madrid from Ireland the code is 07353. From the USA and Canada it's 071, while from Australia and New Zealand it's 0761. Telephone numbers that begin with 900 are free but can't be dialled from abroad.

As well as public phone boxes (*cabinas*) most bars have payphones. There is a high minimum connection charge for international calls, so ensure you have plenty of coins on hand. Avoid phoning from your hotel room if you can – the rates charged are often exorbitant.

GUIDED TOURS OF LA LATINA

La Latina is one of the oldest and most charming parts of Madrid, with its steep, narrow streets lined with tall, elegant houses, and its old-fashioned bars. You can visit the district with an English or Spanish-speaking guide at a cost of around €3 per person. For full information, contact:

Tourist Information Office
Plaza Mayor, 3
☎ 91 588 16 36

BUS TOURS

You can get a good overall picture of the city by taking a guided tour by bus. The commentaries are often

OPENING TIMES

You'll need to look out for museum opening times. There really isn't any rule, apart from the fact that the majority are closed on Monday (Prado, Thyssen-Bornemisza, Lazaro Galdiano, etc.) and many are also closed on Sunday afternoons. Check the opening times carefully before making your visit as they can sometimes change without warning.

THE BONO MUSEO CARD

For art lovers or anyone who's decided to spend a cultural weekend in the museums, the Bono Museo card is invaluable. It can be bought at the entrance to the Centro Cultural Reina Sofía, the Prado or the Museo Thyssen-Bornemisza and is valid for all three museums.

given in several languages. Tours leave Gran Via 32 from 9.45am to 5.15pm and cost around €10 per adult.

For more information, call ☎ 91 302 45 26 or 91 767 17 43.

TOURIST INFORMATION OFFICES

The web site of the Spanish tourist information office (www.tourspain.es) is a mine of information about transport, museums, hotels, cultural life, etc.

Maps of the city and information about guided tours, shows, etc., are available from all tourist information offices. The main offices can be found at:

Plaza Mayor, 3
☎ 91 588 16 36
Mon.-Fri. 10am-8pm,
Sat. 10am-2pm.

Calle Duque de Medinaceli, 2
☎ 91 429 49 51
Mon.-Fri. 10am-8pm,
Sat. 10am-1pm.

Mercado Puerta de Toledo
Ronda de Toledo
☎ 91 364 18 76
Mon.-Fri. 9am-7pm,
Sat. 9.30am-2pm

Barajas Airport
☎ 91 305 86 56
Mon.-Fri. 8am-8pm,
Sat. 9am-1pm.

Estación de Chamartín
(in main hall of the station)
☎ 91 315 99 76
Mon.-Fri. 8am-8pm,
Sat. 9am-1pm.

EXCURSIONS

The area around Madrid holds a number of treasures for those who have time to explore it (see also coloured section).

Aranjuez (47km/29 miles from Madrid). The city is worth a visit, especially for its royal palace, which was the residence of the kings from the 15th century onwards. Trains leave every 30 minutes from Atocha station, with a special tourist train running from May to October. For tourist information, call ☎ 91 891 04 27.

El Escorial (50km/31 miles from Madrid). You'll fall under the spell of this majestic group of buildings. As well as a monastery, it includes a palace, a basilica (crowned with a 92m/300ft dome) and a library boasting over 40,000 volumes and manuscripts, the oldest of which date from the 9th century. There are trains from Atocha and Chamartín stations. For tourist information, call ☎ 91 890 15 54.

Segovia (87km/54 miles from Madrid). The city is renowned for its Roman aqueduct, cathedral, churches and the Alcázar. There are trains from Atocha station at regular intervals and buses from the Paseo de la Florida. For tourist information, call ☎ 921 46 00 34.

Toledo (70km/44 miles from Madrid). An imposing city imbued with the spirit of El Greco. There are regular trains from Atocha station, and buses from Estación Sur. For tourist information, call ☎ 925 22 08 43.

Greenery and culture in the Prado district

In the 18th century, Carlos III decided to expand Madrid to give it a layout worthy of a capital city. Once the wide avenue, the Paseo del Prado was built, it soon became the haunt of the high society of the day. This avenue was extended in the 19th century into the Paseo de la Castellana. These *paseos*, lined with shady paths and embellished with gardens, monumental fountains and grand squares have remained prestigious places. The remains of the Buen Retiro, the old royal palace, now house museums.

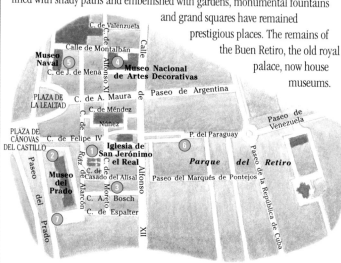

❶ Iglesia de San Jerónimo el Real★★
Calle Moreto, 4
☎ 91 420 35 78
Daily 9am-1pm, 5-8.30pm.

This church was originally built in the 16th century as part of a monastery, the ruins of which can still be seen beside it. It was the symbolic setting for the marriage of King Alfonso XIII and for the coronation of Juan Carlos I after the death of Franco.

It was given a neo-Gothic makeover in the 19th century, and is now considered one of the finest churches in Madrid.

❷ Museo del Prado★★★
Paseo del Prado
☎ 91 330 28 00
or 91 330 29 00
Tue.-Sat. 9am-7pm, Sun. and hols. 9am-2pm
Entry charge, except Sat. afternoon and Sun.

This museum, housing true masterpieces of European painting from the Middle Ages to the 20th century, is simply unmissable. As well as the Spanish school, there are Flemish and Italian works of outstanding interest.

The extraordinary collection of works by Velázquez is quite remarkable for its portraits, as well as the mythological and religious subjects, and the paintings by El Greco are very impressive. Italy is represented by Tintoretto, Veronese and Titian, while the Flemish school is identified by the frenzied compositions of Bosch. The Cason del Buen Retiro museum, an annexe of the Prado, houses a collection of historical works.

❸ Santa Clara★
Calle Moreto, 17
☎ **91 420 07 65**
Sun.-Fri. noon-1.30pm.

The ideal place to stop for a break

between museums, especially if you sit out on the terrace and order some of the tapas and *pinchos* for which it's renowned. This will make your rest even more enjoyable.

❹ Museo Nacional de Artes Decorativas★★★
Calle Montalbán, 12
☎ **91 532 64 99**
Tue.-Fri. 9.30am-3pm (2.30 in summer),
Sat.-Sun. 10am-2pm
Entry charge (except senior citizens).

This museum is home to an array of beautiful *objets d'art* and furniture, including a Sèvres porcelain vase that was a gift from Napoleon III to Isabel II, a Murano glass crib, a collection of doll's houses and a superb example of an 18th-century Valencian kitchen.

❺ Museo Naval★
Paseo del Prado, 5
☎ **91 379 52 99**
Tue.-Sun. 10.30am-1.30pm
Entry free.

Answer the call of the sea and immerse yourself in this museum. Don't leave without seeing the first map ever to show America. It was drawn by Juan de la Cosa, a travelling companion of Christopher Colombus, on his return to Spain.

❻ Parque del Retiro★★
☎ **91 573 62 45**
Every day, 24hrs.

This park really lives up to its name, which means 'retreat'. A haven of greenery in the heart of Madrid, it's the ideal place to come if you're looking for a relaxing stroll. With its fortune tellers, puppeteers, musicians, painters and

traders of every kind, it has an atmosphere all of its own on Sunday mornings. You can take a boat out on the lake or wander round the Palacio de Cristal, constructed by Ricardo Velázquez Bosco from iron and glass, and adorned with colourful azulejos (glazed ceramic tiles) by Daniel Zuloaga.

❼ EL PABELLÓN GOYA★★★
Inside the Prado Museum, Murillo Door
Same opening hours as museum.

Goya: The Naked Maja

These rooms, first opened in 1999, house a collection of 18th-century Spanish paintings centred on the works of Goya. Don't miss the famous *El Tres de Mayo* (The Third of May), in which Goya depicts his vision of a land torn apart by war between the *Madrileños* and the mercenaries of General Murat. The condemned man's gesture of defiance is very moving.

A bit of culture in Banco de España

If you look carefully at the street names and the commemorative plaques in this area, you'll realise you're in the centre of the literary Madrid of the 17th century. Seek out the Golden Age of Castilian literature by retracing the footsteps of such notable authors as Cervantès, Lope de Vega, Cadalso, Morantín and others. The Zarzuela theatre is still here, as are the palaces that line the Paseo del Prado.

❶ Museo Thyssen-Bornemisza★★★
Paseo del Prado, 8
☎ 91 420 39 44
Tue.-Sun. 10am-7pm
Entry charge.

Since 1992 the Palacio de Villahermosa has housed the stunning art collection belonging to Baron Heinrich Thyssen-Bornemisza and his son Hans Heinrich. The eight hundred or so superbly-displayed works representing European painting from the 13th to the 20th century and the sheer scale of the museum make it a must for art lovers. Nearly 18,000m² (195,000 sq ft) of galleries contain masterpieces from the German School (Dürer), Flemish School (Van Eyck and Rubens), Italian School (Canaletto and Guardi) and Dutch School, as well as works by the French Impressionists (Renoir and Van Gogh) and the avant-garde painting of the Fauvists and Cubists (Picasso), the Russians (Kandinsky) and the Pop Art of North America.

❷ Taberna de Dolores★★
Plaza de Jesús, 4
☎ 91 429 22 43
Every day 11-1am.

Even if the Taberna de Dolores wasn't renowned for its *pulgas* (canapés of roquefort cheese and anchovy or tomato and anchovy), the mosaic shop front alone would make you want to try it out. It's quiet at lunchtime and lively in the evening, so choose your time carefully.

❸ Casa de Lope de Vega★
Calle Cervantes, 11
☎ **91 429 92 16**
**Tue.-Fri. 9.30am-2pm,
Sat. 10am-1.30pm,
closed Aug.
Entry charge
except Wed.
Guided tour
in Spanish
obligatory.**

This house,
dating from the
17th century, was
home to the famous
Spanish playwright Felix Lope
de Vega. The interior and the
garden have been reconstructed
to match the description he
gave of them in his works.
Some of the furniture
belonged to Lope de Vega
himself, and the chapel,
office-cum-library and
'platform', the 17th-century
women's sitting room, have a
particular charm.

❹ Almacén de Licores★★
**Calle Cervantes, 6
Mon.-Fri.
10am-2pm, 5-8pm,
Sat. 10am-2pm.**

The owner of this
establishment chalks
his menu over the
walls next door.
You'll find a
good choice of
liqueurs, from
the traditional
Pacharan to
the *turrón*
liqueurs, with
hazelnut,
cinnamon,
peach and
apricot flavours.
If you've never
indulged, take
this opportunity
to give them a try.

❺ Casa de las Escayolas★★
**Shop: Calle de León, 5
Warehouse (open to public):
Calle Cervantes, 3**
☎ **91 429 48 50**
**Mon.-Fri. 9.30am-2pm,
5-8.30pm, Sat. 10am-2pm.**

Don't miss this Aladdin's cave
if you're a DIY enthusiast.
You'll find everything here
you need for painting and
paint effects, as well as a
whole host of objects made of
plaster, resin and wood to try
your handiwork on, including
lampstands, photo frames
and figurines to decorate
according to your taste.

❻ Cafe du Circulo de Bellas Artes★★★
**Calle del Marqués de
Casa Riera, 2**
☎ **91 360 51 00**
Every day 9-1am.

This café, which is used to
house temporary exhibitions,
is more like an old-fashioned
club. The vast room, wooden
floors, bay
windows
which
overlook
the Gran
Vía, the
Calle
Alcala
and the
Plaza de
Cibeles,
and its giant
ceiling frescoes
and fabulous chandeliers
give the place an elegant
atmosphere in which to relax
and soak up the ambiance.

❼ PLAZA DE CIBELES★

You'll find the Plaza
de Cibeles at the cross-
roads of the Gran Via
and the Calle de Alcal.
In the centre stands the
monumental fountain
commissioned by Carlos
III in the 18th century,
depicting the goddess
Cybele enthroned on a
chariot drawn by two
lions. It looks magnificent
at night when it's illuminated. Around the square
are the head offices of the
Spanish institutions –
the main post office, the
Ministry of Defence and
the Bank of Spain, which
has lent its name to the
nearest metro station.

The theatres and bars of Plaza Santa Ana

Built on the former site of a Carmelite convent, today the square forms the centre of a district that is liveliest at night. The statue of Calderón contemplates the façade of the Teatro Español, the city's oldest theatre, which was famous in the 16th and 17th centuries for its great premières. The district is still home to most of the theatres in Madrid.

Map labels: C. de la Aduana · Real Academia de Bellas Artes de San Fernando ❸ · Alcalá · Calle de · C. de Sevilla · Carrera de · PLAZA DE CANALEJAS · S. Jerónimo · C. de Espoz y Mina · Cruz · del Príncipe · Echegaray · C. de la · C. de Nuñez de Arce · C. M. y Gonzáles · C. de Carretas · Iglesia de Santa Cruz · PL. DE JACINTO BENAVENTE ❺ · PLAZA DE SANTA ANA · Calle del Prado · ❹ · C. de C. Jerónima ❼ · Calle del Doctor Cortezo · Calle · PLAZA DEL ANGEL ❻ · León · ❽ · Calle · ❷ · Calle de las Huertas · Atocha · C. de Cañizares · Antón Martín Ⓜ · ❶

❶ Casa Alberto★★
Calle Huertas, 18
☎ 91 429 93 56
Tue.-Sat. 1-4pm, 9pm-midnight, Sun. 1-4pm.

The warm wood panelling on the walls of this tavern have seen 177 years of patronage. If this feast for the eyes isn't enough on its own, you can nibble away on some delicious tapas at the bar or tuck into something a little more substantial in the dining room, which is decorated with lively posters depicting typical scenes of bullfighting.

❷ Parroquia San Sebastián★
Calle Atocha, 39
☎ 91 429 13 61
Every day 9.30am-1pm, 5-8pm.
Entry free.

In the 17th and 18th centuries, all the important ceremonies in Madrid, such as weddings and funerals, took place in this church, which has been declared a historical and artistic monument. Its neo-baroque façade, which was given a neo-Classical makeover in 1829, has helped to make it famous.

❸ Real Academia de Bellas Artes de San Fernando★★★
Calle Alcalá, 13
☎ 91 522 14 91

Tue.-Fri. 9am-7pm, Sat.-Sun. 9am-2.30pm
Entry charge.

Since 1744, the Academy of Fine Arts has been housed in the former palace of Juan de Goyeneche. It contains an important collection of 16th to 18th-century sculptures and works by such artists as El Greco, Velázquez, Rubens and Van Dyck. Don't miss the paintings of the Golden Age, especially *Fray Jerónimo Pérez* by Zurbarán and *San Diego Feeding the Poor* by Murillo.

❹ Viva Madrid★★★
Calle Manuel Fernández y González, 7
☎ 91 429 36 40
Every day 1pm-2am.

As the hours go by, the music gets louder, turning this quiet daytime tapas bar into a *copas* bar from 7pm onwards.

It's located in a *callejon* (a place where tramcars are parked). From the terrace, which is open in summer, there is a marvellous view of the magnificent coloured azulejo columns on the front of the bar.

❺ Chopo★
Plaza del Angel, 15
☎ 91 369 02 77
Mon.-Fri. 10am-2pm, 5-8pm, Sat. 10am-2pm.

This shop is dedicated to all budding artists, DIY enthusiasts and anyone else who loves making things. You'll find all the materials you could possibly need here, including wooden flowers, mosaics, lampstands and trays, as well as plaster masks and figurines to paint, varnish or decorate with a special effect. Don't be afraid to ask the assistants for advice.

❻ Villa Rosa★★★
Plaza Santa Ana, 5
☎ 91 521 36 89
Mon.-Sat. 11pm-5am.

As the night wears on, the more packed this disco-bar gets and the livelier the atmosphere becomes. The regulars come here to dance the night away after doing the rounds of the local bars. The walls are covered inside and out with azulejo tiles and the Moorish decor is quite spectacular. Cult film director,

Pedro Almodóvar, who was an important figure in the *movida*, shot some scenes from *High Heels* here, so if you're a film buff, you really wouldn't want to miss it.

❼ Iglesia de Santa Cruz★
Calle Atocha, 6
☎ 91 639 12 39
Every day 9.30-11am.

This church was built in a neo-Gothic style according to plans drawn up by the Marquis of Cuba. You'll be able to admire the building's very fine choir, as well as its numerous chapels. With works by the painter Alonso Cano and the sculptor Salvador Carmona, the museum is also worth seeing (entry charge).

❽ Los Gabrieles★★★
Calle Echegaray, 17
☎ 91 429 62 61
Every day 12.30pm-2am.

This was one of the best-known bars of the post-war period, the time of Manolete, the famous bull-fighter, and Ava Gardner. During the daytime, the atmosphere is quiet and you can eat your tapas in peace. Later, however, the music starts, the tapas disappear and it's time for a *vinito* (wine) or *caña* (beer). Look out for the superbly-restored azulejo tiles.

Puerta del Sol, the forum of Madrid

On the site of the eastern medieval gate, the Puerta del Sol is said to be the starting-point of all the roads in Spain and is the place where the main roads of Madrid converge. Semicircular in shape, it was here that the people of Madrid resisted Napoleon's troops. It was also the scene of revolts in 1820 and the proclamation of the republic in 1931. A bronze statue of the city's emblem, the bear reaching for the fruit of a *madroño* (strawberry tree), has pride of place. An advertisement for Tío Pepe, declared as a historical monument, looks down from the roof of one of the buildings.

Gran Vía Ⓜ

Calle de la Montera

PLAZA DEL CARMEN

Calle del Carmen

C. de la Aduana

Calle de Alcalá

C. de Preciados

PLAZA DE LAS DESCALZAS

Calle del Arenal

C. de Tetuán

Iglesia San Ginés

P. de San Ginés

Sol Ⓜ PL. DE LA PUERTA DEL SOL

C. de San Jerónimo

PLAZA DE CANALEJAS

Mayor

C. de E. y Mina

C. de la Cruz

C. Correo

C. de Carretas

C. M. V. de Pontejos

Calle

PLAZA MAYOR

C. C. de Miranda

PL. DEL CONDE DE MIRANDA

C. de Toledo

C. Pasa

❶ Plaza Mayor ★★★

As you emerge from one of the narrow passages that open onto Plaza Mayor, the sight of the vast square will take your breath away. Felipe II commissioned a design by Juan de Herrera, the architect of El Escorial palace, but Felipe III (whose statue stands in the centre of the square) chose a design by Juan Gomez de Mora. The beautiful Casa de la Panadería (baker's) and Casa de la Carnicería (butcher's) are reminders of the sizeable original market.

Plaza Mayor was the site of the canonisation of San Isidro, the patron saint of the city, as well as large numbers of executions, tournaments and bullfights. The wedding of Isabel II was also celebrated here in 1846. Nowadays the Christmas market is held under the arcades, while on Sunday mornings, there's a stamp and coin market. As soon as the weather turns fine, the café terraces attract the crowds.

❷ Monjas Jerónimas del Monasterio del Corpus Christi ★

Plaza del Conde de Miranda, 3
☎ **91 548 37 01**
Every day 9am-1pm.

How can you indulge yourself but still feel that you are doing a good deed? The answer is to buy some of the traditional patisserie (including the delicious *pastas de almendra y de té* and *naranjines*) made and sold by four of the sisters of this convent. Set back from a little square, the convent itself also houses a fine altarpiece that's worth going out of your way to see (every day 1.30-2pm, 7-8pm).

❸ La Violeta★
Plaza de Canalejas, 6
☎ **91 522 55 22**
**Mon.-Sat. 9.30am-2pm,
4.30-8.30pm.**

A little turn-of-the-century shop specialising in violet sweets. They have the colour, flavour and shape of violets and are famous the world over. They can only be found here and are quite delicious. You can bring them back in glass bottles or buy them in attractive gift packs.

❹ Lhardy★★
Carrera de San Jerónimo, 8
☎ **91 522 22 07**
**Mon.-Sat. 9.30am-3pm,
5-9.30pm, closed Aug.**

The restaurant, established in 1839, is on the first floor, but it's really much more fun to stand at the counter downstairs and eat the speciality of the house, the *croquetas* (croquettes), while they're still nice and hot. In winter, try the renowned and warming *caldo* (broth). If you prefer more traditional fare, you can order delicious pastries made with sweetened dough or sandwiches with your coffee or beer.

❺ Manzana★
Plaza del Carmen, 3
☎ **91 521 40 61**
**Mon.-Sat. 10.15am-2pm,
5-8.30pm.**

A little specialised record shop where you'll find the best of the hot rhythms – Latin music, with Willy Chirino and La Charanga Habanera, African music, with Ismaël Lo and Angelique Kidjo, and Algerian Raï music performed by Khaled.

❻ La Metralleta★
Plaza de las Descalzas
☎ **91 532 52 24**
**Mon.-Sat. 10am-2.30pm,
4.30-8.30pm.**

Music lovers of every kind will really appreciate this handy shop. To quote the words of the sales assistant, the prices are *really* slashed. Music of every genre and every period is bought and sold here secondhand.

❼ Iglesia San Ginés★★
Calle Arenal, 13
☎ **91 366 48 75**
**Mon.-Sun.
9am-1pm, 6-9pm.**

This small Baroque church was built in 1645 on the ruins of one of the oldest churches in Madrid. It was the result of a papal edict issued by Pope Innocent VI and the plans were drawn up by Juan Ruiz. It contains very fine paintings by Salvatierra, El Greco, Alonso Cano, Juan de Porres and many others.

❽ Monasterio de las Descalzas Reales★★★
Plaza de las Descalzas, 3
☎ **91 454 87 00**
**Tue.-Thu. and Sat. 10.30am-12.45pm, 4-5.45pm,
Fri. 10.30am-12.45pm,
Sun. and holidays 11am-1.45pm**
Entry charge.

PUERTA DEL SOL ON THE EVENING OF 'NOCHE VIEJA'

On 'Noche Vieja', or New Year's Eve, countless numbers of *Madrileños* gather in the Puerta del Sol. According to tradition, they all have to swallow a grape on each of the twelve strokes of midnight in order to bring luck for the new year. The celebrations then begin in earnest and the *cava* flows freely. There's always a great atmosphere, so don't miss out if you're in Madrid for New Year.

9 Casa Labra★★
Calle Tetuán, 12
☎ 91 532 14 05
Every day 11am-
3.30pm, 5.30-1pm.

This bar has changed little since it opened in 1860. If you come in through the right-hand door, you'll soon see the kind of food that's served here. It consists of croquettes of cod or tuna and tomato – and nothing else. But when they're washed down with a *caña* (beer), they're worth coming for.

10 Palacio de Gaviria★★★
Calle Arenal, 9
☎ 91 526 60 69
Mon.-Sat. 10.30pm-3am,
Sun. 8pm-2am.

Currently occupied by a community of Poor Clares, this monastery was built in the 16th century by Doña Juana, daughter of Emperor Charles V (Carlos I of Spain). It was used for a long time as a retreat by people of noble birth who wished to retire from the world. Over the years, their families donated gifts, such as precious boxes and chests, that swelled the museum's collection. The monastery has an extraordinary staircase decorated with frescoes that opens onto a pretty gallery lined with chapels on the first floor. Besides superb paintings by Zurbarán, Rubens, Titian and Brueghel the Elder, there are very fine 17th-century tapestries executed to designs by Rubens. It is worth visiting just to see these.

In the 19th century the Marquis of Gaviria used this palace to host lavish receptions. The magnificent entrance sets the tone, which continues with a number of richly-decorated small sitting rooms and boudoirs on the first floor. Nowadays you can dance to techno music or sway to the sound of South American rhythms in the mirrored hall, learn to tango (on Wednesdays), play billiards or, as in any other

bar, simply have a drink – except that you'll be in a palace! It's become an essential part of the *Madrileño* night out.

⓫ Sanatorio de Muñecas★
Calle de Preciados, 21
☎ 91 521 04 47
Mon.-Sat. 10am-8.30pm.

Don't worry if your favourite doll has lost a finger, an eye or even her hair. Whether she's old or new, made of porcelain or plastic, just bring her along to this doll's hospital and she'll be 'cured' on the spot. Among the excellent variety of other toys, the shop boasts a very fine collection of lead soldiers, all handpainted by the artist Javier Barrientos.

⓬ Casa Mira★★
Carrera de San Jerónimo, 30
☎ 91 429 67 96
**Every day
9.30am-2pm, 4.30-9pm.**

If you like *turrón* (nougat), don't miss this shop, which is especially popular with *Madrileños* at Christmas time. Since 1842, Luis Mira and his successors have been making Spanish sweet specialities the traditional way. It goes without saying that their home-made *turrón* bears very little resemblance to that found in super-markets. Not to mention

the wide variety of flavours available, including hazelnut, candied fruit, chocolate and coconut.

⓭ Pasage del Comercio
Calle de la Montera, 33

This passage, allowing direct access to Calle Tres Cruces is like a haven of peace in this lively district. The wrought iron decorations over the doors, fine ochre and neutral-coloured façades, mouldings on the windowsills and *trompe-l'œil* effects on the walls all ensure it oozes charm. It's a pity there isn't a bar in sight!

⓮ Chocolatería San Ginés★★
Pasadizo de San Ginés, 5
Every day 10pm-7am.

With its bottle-green walls decorated with mirrors, this charming chocolate house is for those who like to stay up late. This is where you'll

find *Madrileño* night-owls who have come to end their evening with *chocolate con churros* before returning home to bed – of course you could just get up early!

⓯ El Arco de los Cuchilleros★
Plaza Mayor, 9
☎ 91 365 26 80
**Mon.-Sat. 11am-9pm,
Sun. in autumn and winter
11am-8pm.**

Among the familiar and more unusual objects on offer, the ceramic pieces are worth noting for their originality and modern designs. They include floral patterned and blue-and-white checked teapots, cubic tea sets and brightly-coloured storage jars.

THE LAST OF THE OLD-FASHIONED SHOE-SHINERS

Take the opportunity to stroll along Gran Via, which was built under the dictatorship of Primo de Rivera. It isn't of any great artistic interest with its pompously heavy and imposing architecture, however, dotted along the avenue you'll still find a few old-fashioned shoe-shiners at work. It's not often you get the chance to have your shoes spruced up while you have a rest after so much walking.

Palacio Real and the Austrian district

A s a royal city and European capital, Madrid owes much of its importance to the Holy Roman Emperor Charles V (Carlos I of Spain) and the House of Austria. Lost in admiration at the sight of the city, the emperor had the Alcázar rebuilt and fitted out the present royal palace. Aristocratic families close to the Habsburgs settled in the city and Felipe II even decided to move the capital of his kingdom to Madrid after he succeeded his father.

❶ Palacio Real★★★

Calle de Bailén
☎ 91 454 87 00
Mon.-Sat. 9.30am-5pm,
Sun. and holidays 9am-2pm.

Built in 1734, after the fire at the Alcázar, the vast and extravagant royal palace is now a storehouse of treasures. To reach the first floor, take the grand staircase, in one of the finest parts of the building, with its lavish painted ceiling. Here you'll find the 'Saleta Gasparini', housing Goya's portrait of Carlos IV, followed by the Throne Room, with its vault decorated by Tiepolo and the grand dining room.

❷ Monasterio de la Encarnación★

Plaza de la Encarnación, 1
☎ 91 454 87 00
Tue.-Thu. and Sat. 10.30am-12.45pm, 4-5.45pm,
Fri. 10.30am-12.45pm, Sun. and holidays 11am-1.45pm.

Founded in 1611 by Margaret of Austria, wife of Felipe III, this convent stands in a square not far from the Cabo Noval gardens. It houses portraits of the House of Bourbon and an impressive collection of relics, including a phial of dried blood of St Pantaleon, said to liquify on the anniversary of the saint's death. The main cloister is quite beautiful.

❸ Plaza de Oriente★★

Easily located by the statue of Felipe IV at its centre, the Plaza de Oriente is remarkable for its simple architecture. Once an important venue for state occasions, everything about the square contributes to its nobility, from its views of the Palacio Real and the Teatro Real, to the royal statues lining its sides. It's become even more pleasant since it's been closed to traffic.

4 Café de Oriente★★

Plaza de Oriente, 2
☎ 91 541 39 74
Every day
1-4pm, 9pm-midnight.

Although built on the remains of an old convent, this café is far from austere. On the contrary, its four dining rooms have an atmosphere full of real charm and warmth. In spring and summer you can enjoy a great view of the Palacio Real while enjoying tapas or lunch on the terrace.

If you've ever dreamt of dressing up as a flamenco dancer, this shop is definitely the place for you. With the elaborate dresses, dance outfits, accessories, musical instruments and, above all, CDs and records of flamenco music on offer, you'll find everything you could possibly need here.

A smart and original bar housed in a marvellous vaulted cellar. Built on the site of the old city walls, there are windows in the floor so that you can view the excavations and the ancient vases below. Everything in the bar is decorated in shades of red ochre, and they serve a wide variety of cocktails and coffee.

5 Taberna del Alabardero★★

Calle Felipe V, 6
☎ 91 547 25 77
Every day 8.30-1am.

This tapas bar is owned by the same people as the Café de Oriente and it's every bit as charming, but on a more simple note. You can stand at the bar or sit at one of the few wooden tables and order *montaditos* and other tasty snacks. Add a *vinito* or a *caña* to complete the experience.

6 El Flamenco Vive★★

Calle Conde de Lemos, 7
☎ 91 547 39 17
Mon.-Sat. 10.30am-2pm, 5-9pm.

7 Museo Cerralbo★★

Calle Ventura Rodríguez, 17
☎ 91 547 36 46
Tue.-Sat. 9.30am-2.30pm, Sun. 10am-2pm.

This small 19th-century Italianate palace was once owned by the Marquis of Cerralbo, who presented it to the State in 1924. Declared a historical and artistic monument in 1962, its lavish rooms house a wealth of exhibits including sculptures, tapestries, porcelain and European and Japanese weaponry. Painting is also represented, with works by El Greco, Zurbarán, Van Dyck, Tintoretto, Titian and Goya.

8 El Aljibe★★

Calle Carlos III, 3 (basement)
☎ 91 548 46 20
Every day 7pm-3am.

9 PLAZA DE LA VILLA

This quiet pedestrian square is surrounded by some of the most historic administrative buildings in the city. The Casa de la Villa houses the town hall and is linked to the 16th-century Casa Cisneros by an enclosed bridge. Take a look at its elaborate façade, built in a Plateresque style. Legend has it that after the Battle of Pavia, François I of France was imprisoned in the Torre de Lujanes, the oldest building in the square, built entirely of brick and plaster in the early 15th century.

La Latina and the Rastro, bargains and tertulia

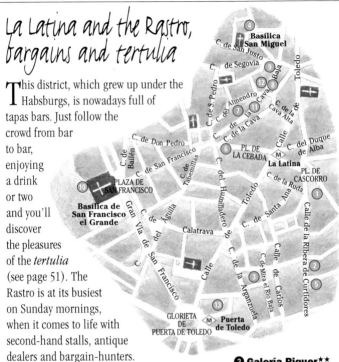

This district, which grew up under the Habsburgs, is nowadays full of tapas bars. Just follow the crowd from bar to bar, enjoying a drink or two and you'll discover the pleasures of the *tertulia* (see page 51). The Rastro is at its busiest on Sunday mornings, when it comes to life with second-hand stalls, antique dealers and bargain-hunters.

❷ Galería Piquer★★
Calle Ribera de Curtidores, 29
Mon.-Fri. 11am-2pm, 5-8pm,
Sat.-Sun. 11am-2pm.

Thirty or so high-quality antique shops are grouped here, selling traditional furniture and *objets d'art*, as well as more exotic items. Most of the pieces come from

❶ Rastro★
Calle Ribera de Curtidores
and surrounding streets
Sun. and holidays 9am-2pm.

The Rastro is a Sunday ritual if ever there was one. It's one of the city's great institutions and the flea markets of other cities pale in comparison. Every Sunday the streets are the scene of a grand trading frenzy as a tide of human beings sweeps through them searching for a bargain. You can buy just about anything here – books, old furniture, second-hand clothes, wrought iron work, ceramics, pet food and anything else you care to mention. You certainly won't come away empty-handed.

England's quality antique furniture trade, so prices aren't necessarily cheap. However, window shopping is completely free.

❸ El Transformista★
Calle Mira el Rio Baja, 18
☎ 91 539 88 33
Tue.-Sun. 11am-2pm.

Located in the heart of the Rastro, you'll have to delve about in this establishment amongst the old baroque mirrors, lamps and antique vases to find what you're looking for. If you don't see anything you like, take a look in the surrounding streets (Calle Carlos Arniches and Calle del Carnero), where most of the second-hand shops can be found.

❹ Basílica San Miguel★
Calle de San Justo, 4
☎ 91 548 40 11
Every day 10am-2pm, 5.30-9pm.

Built with the financial assistance of the Archbishop of Toledo, Cardinal Infante Luis de Bourbon, this basilica, with its narrow Italian baroque façade, is one of the loveliest in Madrid. It houses some fine sculptures by Roberto Michel and Salvador Carmona, as well as paintings by Ferrante and Velázquez.

❺ Albarrelo★★
Calle Ribera de Curtidores, 12 Local 50
☎ 91 528 08 24
Mon.-Fri. 11am-2pm 5-8pm, Sat.-Sun. 11am-2pm.

This elegant shop sells both reproductions of 19th-century Spanish ceramics and classic contemporary works. Whether you choose a small box, a plate or a liqueur decanter with a set of four matching glasses (around €60), this is the ideal place to come to find an original and attractive souvenir of your stay in Madrid.

❻ El Viajero★★
Plaza de la Cebada, 11
☎ 91 366 90 64
Tue.-Sat. 12.30pm-1.30am, Sun. 1-7pm.

El Viajero is another place, like the Rastro, that's become popular with the inhabitants of the city. With its modern, metallic decor, you could almost be in New York. Come here for lunch, or just stop off for a drink on your way to sample Cava Baja's numerous tapas bars. The roof terrace has one of the best views of Madrid and is definitely an advantage on hot evenings.

7 TABERNA
ALMENDRO★★★
Calle Almendro, 13
☎ 91 365 42 52
**Wed.-Sun. 1-4pm,
7pm-midnight.**

After visiting the Rastro, this tavern is the ideal place to stop for a break. It's a chance to see the beautiful frescoes inside and to try the local specialities – wines from the south and *roscas*, small crowns of bread used to make sandwiches (meat or charcuterie).

8 Xiquena★★
Calle Cava Baja, 19
☎ 91 366 49 69
**Tue.-Sun. 12.30-4pm,
8pm-midnight.**

Xiquena is both a bar and a shop, which means you can taste a very wide range of Spanish wines while sampling the tapas here. At the rear, you can buy the best type of ham, *jamón ibérico de bellota*, as well as a selection of Spanish cheeses. It's a good place for gourmets to find regional specialities.

9 Fabrica
de churros★
Calle Cava Baja, 7.

As its name suggests, in this shop they make *churros*, the long doughnuts that are so popular with the people of Madrid. Even if you aren't in time to watch the *churros* being made (until around 11am), you can still have a look inside and admire the walls decorated with beautiful azulejo tiles.

10 Basílica
de San
Francisco
el Grande★★
**Plaza de San
Francisco**
☎ 91 365 38 00

**Tues.-Sat. 11am-1pm,
4-6.30pm (8pm in summer)
Guided tour in Spanish
for which there is a small
charge.**

This 18th-century building, dedicated to St Francis of Assisi, is one of the most majestic in the capital. Its imposing size and 32m/105ft-wide dome have earned it the nickname 'El Grande' and it was used for ceremonies by Franco. The interior is currently being restored, but don't miss the paintings by Velázquez, Zurbarán, Ribera and Goya.

⓫ El Tempranillo★★
Calle Cava Baja, 38
☎ 91 364 15 32
**Every day noon-4pm,
8pm-1am,
closed 10-30 Aug.**

With its warm atmosphere, patinated walls and exposed stonework, you're sure to like this bar. It has an amazing wine list, and if you don't want to stand at the bar, there are a few small tables for you to relax at. The house tapas are both unusual and interesting. Ask for such tempting specialities as *revuelto de hortalizas* (with vegetables) or *mollejas de cordero guisadas* (with lamb).

⓬ Del Hierro★
Calle Cava Baja, 6
☎ 91 364 58 91
**Mon.-Fri. noon-2pm,
6-9pm, closed Sun. except
summer noon-2pm.**

If you're an ardent admirer of the designer Inaki Sempedro, or if, as is perhaps more likely, you're looking for an original and stylish bag, in any shape, colour or material, you may well find what you're looking for in this shop. With a wonderful selection of small bags, large bags, round bags and square bags, clutch bags, evening bags and even holdalls, there are items to suit all tastes and budgets.

⓭ La Oca★
Centro
Comercial
de la
Puerta
de Toledo
**Mon.-Fri.
10am-2pm,
3-8.30pm,
Sat. 10.30am-2.30pm,
5-8pm, Sun. 11.30am-3pm.**

This is an Aladdin's Cave for fans of innovative design. It stocks gadgets, cookware, objects and furniture for every room in the house.

With coasters, corkscrews and soap dishes in bright colours and original shapes, you're sure to find plenty of inspiration for furnishing and decorating ideas. However, be warned, the prices are rather steep.

> #### TERTULIA
>
> Inherited from the oral tradition, *tertulia* is the unique Spanish way of coming together and intellectualising about anything and everything for hours on end. From the more superficial viewpoint of a foreigner, it's also a way of talking without actually saying anything. *Tertulia* is also a physical space, that of the street or café, where social barriers are broken down, conflicts diffused and exchanges of ideas are made easier, but above all, it's conversation and sharing ideas.

Picturesque working-class Lavapiés

With its narrow streets, geranium-covered balconies and washing blowing in the wind, Lavapiés is one of the most picturesque parts of Madrid. The façades were recently restored, trees were planted and the Museum of Contemporary Art opened here in 1986. Yet for all its new lease of life it hasn't lost its working-class roots.

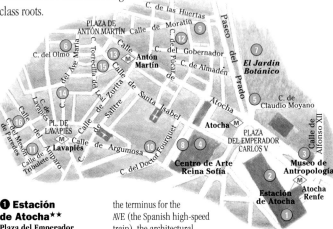

❶ Estación de Atocha★★
Plaza del Emperador Carlos V.

It might seem unusual to visit a station, however, the Estación de Atocha, built according to plans by Gustave Eiffel (of tower fame), is a good example of the late 19th-century style. Converted by Rafael Monero in 1992 as

the terminus for the AVE (the Spanish high-speed train), the architectural elegance of the main cast-iron and glass structures of the exterior were retained. Don't miss the unusual winter garden inside.

❷ Samarkanda★★
**Estación de Atocha
Gta de Carlos V
☎ 91 530 97 46
Every day 1.30-4pm,
9pm-midnight.**

In this colonial-style restaurant, you'll really get the feeling of being in the jungle, with all the cane furniture, parasols, ceiling fans, and a tropical micro-climate into the bargain. It's a fitting place to have a drink and a bite of tapas or

a more substantial meal overlooking the palm trees of the Estación de Atocha's winter garden.

❸ Museo de Antropología★
**Calle Alfonso XII, 68
☎ 91 530 64 18
Tue.-Sat.
10am-7.30pm,
Sun. 10am-2pm
Entry charge.**

This museum houses rich ethnological collections from Asia, Africa, America and Oceania. The diverse objects on display include everyday items such as tools, clothes, weapons, musical instruments, as well as religious and mystical objects such as talismans and carved statues of gods. Don't miss the exhibits from the Philippines – they're quite superb.

4 Centro Cultural Reina Sofía★★★
Calle Santa Isabel, 52
☎ **91 467 50 62**
Mon.-Sat. 10am-9pm,
Sun. 10am-2.30pm
Entry charge except Sat.
2.30-9pm and Sun.

Madrid's old general hospital recently made way for one of the most modern and spacious museums in the country, which was soon nicknamed 'Sofidou', after the Pompidou Centre in Paris, by the locals. The work of Spanish artists of the 19th and 20th centuries (Miró, Tàpies, Picasso, Dalí, López and Arroyo) hangs side by side with work by artists from further afield, such as Calder, Le Corbusier, Arp, Bacon and Ernst. The undoubted gem of the collection is Picasso's famous work, *Guernica* (see page 54). Sculpture is represented by two of the greatest surviving Spanish masters, Jorge de Oteiza and Edouardo Chillida. The centre regularly houses temporary exhibitions and retrospectives of both well-known and relatively unknown artists.

5 Feria del Libro★
Calle Claudio Moyano
Every day 9.30am-2pm.

As you walk alongside the botanical gardens, you'll notice little wooden kiosks similar to those found on the banks of the Seine in Paris, They sell old and antiquarian books and the inhabitants of Madrid love to come here to search through the old comic books, out-of-print volumes and second-hand paperbacks.

6 Kappa★
Calle Olmo, 26
☎ **91 527 08 30**
Mon.-Fri. 8.30pm-3am,
Sat.-Sun. 1pm-4am.

You can't miss the window display full of pebbles decorated with whirling dervishes – and you don't get much more unusual than that! Open every evening, the bar throbs to the sound of dance music (techno, house, jungle, etc.) and only really gets going after midnight.

7 Jardín Botánico★★★
Paseo del Prado
Every day 10am-6pm
(later in summer)
Entry charge.

With 30,000 species of plants, this garden, running the length of the Paseo del Prado, is a haven of peace and tranquillity. The benches dotted here and there are invitations to pause a while and contemplate. Designed in 1781 for King Carlos III, it's wonderful to walk here in spring, when the trees and shrubs are in blossom. The Palacio Villanueva houses temporary exhibitions.

⑧ GUERNICA★★★

This gigantic painting, dedicated to the martyred Basque town of Guernica, was Picasso's angry reaction to its destruction by German bombers supporting the Francoist forces in the Spanish Civil War. Then director of the Prado, he combined the mythology of the Minotaur with the theme of the massacre of the innocents in a vast canvas. The dark colours of mourning contrast with the white of lost purity, forming an oppressive scene. Since its return from the United States and a short stay in the Cason del Buen Retiro, the work can now be seen, surrounded by sketches, in the Centro Cultural Reina Sofía.

⑨ La Platería★
Calle Moratín, 49
☎ 91 429 17 22
Every day 7.30-1am.

This elegant little bistro, a stone's throw from the Paseo del Prado, is pleasantly located in a quiet little square. Tables and chairs appear on the terrace as soon as the weather turns fine. Especially delicious here are the regional charcuterie of Castille and León and the goat's cheese served on bread flavoured with tomato.

⑩ Cristina Guisado★
Calle Doctor Fourquet, 10
☎ 91 528 87 88
Mon.-Sat. 11am-2pm, 5-8.30pm.

If you look back to the 60s and 70s with nostalgia, this shop run by the Guisado sisters is for you. It sells a whole range of original clothes from the period, as well as some amazing accessories, including hats, bags and kipper ties. It's also a good place to come if you're planning a fancy-dress party.

⑪ Comics El Coleccionista★
Calle Tribulete, 7
☎ 91 530 01 33
Mon.-Fri. 10am-2pm, 5-8.30pm, Sat. 10am-2pm.

Superman, Spiderman and many other super heroes await you in this second-hand bookshop which specialises in 1960s comic books. If you rummage around a bit, you may also come up with comics from the turn of the century. They're in Spanish, of course, but it's a good way to learn the language.

⑫ El Alambique★
Calle Fucar, 7
☎ 91 429 65 63
Mon.-Sat. 1-4.30pm, 7pm-1am.

The two little rooms of this restaurant, with its unusual decorative mix of copper and

¿Qué pasa ahí arriba?

KóKINOS

⓯ El Despertar★★
Calle Torrecilla del Leal, 18
☎ **91 530 80 95**
Every day 7pm-2am.

This is a very welcoming café, perhaps because the furniture was bought second-hand from here and there, or because the owner is always so friendly. An artist himself, he loves to share his interests with others, and so at around 11.30pm on Fridays and Saturdays, he stages jazz concerts, poetry readings and exhibitions.

publicity posters, are very striking. The canapés and salads are equally original. Try the salmon with tartare sauce, mango and cheese.

⓭ La Filmoteca★
Calle Santa Isabel, 3
☎ **91 369 11 25**
Tue.-Sun. 4pm-midnight.

La Filmoteca isn't just for film-lovers, as its name suggests. The elaborate façade of this cinema, in shades of ochre and white, is very attractive and invites everyone to enter. Once inside, you'll find a small bookshop and a bar prettily decorated in blue and white. Do check out the programme though – they only show high-quality films here.

⓮ Nuevo Cafe Barbieri★★
Calle Ave Maria, 45
☎ **91 527 36 58**
Every day 3pm-2am.

This bar has been the meeting-place of inhabitants of the district since 1902. You won't find elaborate decor or cuisine here – in fact it's a little old-fashioned and shabby, and the choice of tapas is limited. The main things on offer, however, are a chat at the bar and a chance to read in peace, away from the hustle and bustle of the city.

⓰ Taberna de Antonio Sanchez★★
Mesón de Paredes, 13
☎ **91 539 78 26**
Mon.-Sat. noon-4pm, 8pm-midnight, Sun. noon-4pm.

The Taberna de Antonio Sanchez is probably one of the oldest bars in Madrid. It's almost a historical monument. A few reminders of its early days still remain, such as an old advertisement for cakes for only 15 *centimos*. A visit here would be a good opportunity to try some delicious *tortilla San Isidro*. It's made with cod and onions and comes highly recommended.

Salamanca and its shops

Salamanca has changed considerably since it was built in the second half of the 19th century by order of Isabel II. Originally designed for the aristocracy, who found the city centre stifling, it owed its first major transformation at the start of the 20th century to the Marquis of Salamanca. The name and a majestic square still remain, but nowadays it's a marvellous shopping district.

❶ Museo Arqueológico Nacional★★
Calle Serrano, 13
☎ 91 577 79 12
Tue.-Sat.
9.30am-8.30pm
Entry charge
except Sat. from
2.30pm and
Sun. and holidays
9.30am-2.30pm.

This museum has exhibits ranging from prehistoric times up to the 19th century. It houses a very fine collection of antiquities excavated from all over the Iberian Peninsular, as well as superb Roman mosaics, Egyptian sarcophagi and a replica of the Altamira caves in Cantabria, decorated with Paleolithic paintings.

❷ Art Box★★
Calle Villanueva, 22
☎ 91 431 67 46
Tue.-Sat. 10.30am-2pm,
5-8.30pm, Mon. 5-8.30pm.

However surprising it may seem, this shop specialises in the sale of artworks using an ultramodern computer program (the 'dealer'). Twenty original works can be displayed on a surface 3m/yds square. All you have to do is click on a screen to see the chosen work appear. Also on sale are original objects inspired by the works of famous artists. These include ties with designs by Andy Warhol and jugs in the style of Picasso.

❸ Vazquez★
Calle Ayala, 11
☎ **91 435 20 44**
Mon.-Fri. 8.30am-8.30pm, Sat. 8.30am-2.30pm.

This timeless *frutería*, which is said to be supplier to queen Sofia, is a veritable feast for the eyes. The shop front is covered in a mouth-watering display of top-quality fruit of every shape, colour and variety.

❹ Jurucha★
Calle Ayala, 19
☎ **91 575 00 98**
Mon.-Sat. 7.30am-11pm.

Don't take any notice of this bar's decor – it's what goes on in the kitchen that counts. Over 45 sorts of *pinchos* – individual portions of tapas – are made here. With crab, cod, chilli or ham, served hot or cold, they're all quite

delicious and are beautifully presented. You really must try the *tortilla de patatas* as well as the stuffed eggs (especially the ones stuffed with prawns).

❺ Estay★
Calle Hermosilla, 46
☎ **91 578 04 70**
Mon.-Sat. 8-1.30am.

OK, you like traditional tapas bars, but you're looking for somewhere a little more comfortable with a more up-to-date decor. Why not try *Estay*? They serve courgettes (zucchini) stuffed with prawns and squid, mushroom and prawn vol-au-vents, and *pinchos* with goat's cheese and honey, which are a sure bet if you can't make up your mind. They even sell the paintings on the walls.

❻ Elena Miro★
Calle Hermosilla, 28
☎ **91 576 24 11**
Mon.-Sat. 10am-2pm, 5-8.30pm.
Don't despair if you shop in the outsize department, you'll find just what you're looking for here.

The clothes in this shop start at UK size 18 and there's everything you could possibly want, from jeans, casual ready-to-wear and sportswear to very dressy outfits.

❼ Velas y Decoración★★
Calle Claudio Coello, 69A
☎ **91 577 91 71**
Mon.-Sat. 10am-2pm, 5-8pm.

Here's a chance to stock up on some candles and candle holders to give your home a warm romantic glow.

There are many highly decorative objects here. The wrought iron chandeliers are very effective, but whatever you prefer, you're sure to find something that will enhance your home or make a lovely gift to take back. Prices for simple candles start at around €1 and the sky's the limit.

8 Y LES DIO ALAS★★
Calle Nuñez de Balboa, 37
☎ **91 576 94 38**
Mon.-Fri. 10am-2pm, Mon., Wed., Fri. 5-8pm, Sat. 11am-2pm.

This clothes shop, for children aged 0 to 12 years, specialises in traditional classic styles. You'll find mainly baby clothes (including handmade sleepsuits and jackets), nightwear, dresses and leather trousers. You can even choose your own style, fabric and colour and order any conceivable type of garment made to measure. A classic nightdress sells for around €24, while a leather dress can be yours for the princely sum of €75.

9 La Trainera★★★
Calle Lagasca, 60
☎ **91 576 80 35 or 91 576 05 75**
Mon.-Sat. 1-4pm, 8pm-midnight. Booking advisable.

With fresh supplies delivered daily from Galicia, this is definitely the best seafood and fish restaurant in Madrid. It has everything you could wish for – the atmosphere of a fisherman's cottage and a marvellous window display of seafood with prices ranging from around €36-42. The house specialities are *salpicon de mariscos* (seafood salad), turbot and grilled sole.

10 Chocolateria Jorge Juan★★
Calle Jorge Juan, 12
☎ **91 577 16 07**
Every day 8am-10pm, closed Sun. 2-5pm.

This former franchise of the famous Valor chocolates of Valencia has been turned into a very pleasant 1900s-style chocolate house. Every conceivable kind of drinking chocolate is on offer, including chocolate with cream and iced chocolate. The chocolate served with *churros* is deliciously thick and smooth, something the house of Valor is famous for.

11 Sybilla★★
Callejon de Jorge Juan, 12
☎ **91 578 13 22**
Mon.-Sat. 10am-2pm, 4-8pm.

In the past, the *callejon* was used to store tramcars but it has since had a face-lift and is now home to a large number of interesting shops, one of which is *Sybilla*. Housed in a loft, it sells stunning but fairly expensive outfits, as well as more affordable accessories and a young line, called Jacomomola.

12 Fundación Juan March★★

Calle Castelló, 77
☎ 91 435 42 40
Mon.-Sat. 10am-2pm,
5.30-9pm, Sun. and holidays
10am-2pm.

In addition to very high quality contemporary art exhibitions, the foundation hosts lectures and seminars. From Monday to Saturday at noon you can also listen to chamber music concerts here. Find out what's on before you go.

13 Boly★★

Calle Don Ramón de la Cruz, 14 (1st floor D)
☎ 91 576 33 32
Mon.-Sat.
10am-2pm, 5-8.30pm.

You may have heard of made-to-measure, but the expression takes on a new meaning here. If you've ever thought of having your bags and shoes covered with a

matching fabric of your choice or having a swimsuit made to your exact requirements (from around €85), you can be sure your every wish will be granted here.

14 Beautiful People★

Calle Goya, 20
☎ 91 431 67 69
Mon.-Sat. 10.30am-2.30pm,
4.30-8.30pm.

At Beautiful People you'll find 300m²/3,000sqft of floor space dedicated to the most fashionable international designers of the day in this shopper's paradise. The prices may be a little on the high side, but you can always indulge in a little window-shopping.

15 La Oreja de Plata★

Calle Jorge Juan, 39
☎ 91 576 39 01
Mon.-Fri. 10.30am-2pm,
5-8.30pm, Sat. 10.30am-2pm.

This recently-opened shop is a choice space for designers who come here from all over the world to showcase their designs. Objects on sale include watches, necklaces, bracelets and ebony inlaid boxes, some of which are limited editions.

16 Trotamundos

Calle Serrano, 81
☎ 91 563 22 21
Mon.-Sat. 10am-2pm,
5-8pm.

You may have seen more or less the same sports and leisure goods on display at *Coronel Tapioca* (see page 97), but the ones you'll find here are seconds, so you will find plenty of bargains. Because they're slightly flawed, they're on sale at unbeatable prices.

17 MERCADO DE LA PAZ★★

Calle Ayala, 28
Mon.-Fri. 8am-3pm,
5.30-8pm, Sat. 8am-3pm.

If you're looking for somewhere lively to do your shopping, you'll find it at this covered market. Make for La Boulette at stands 63 and 68. This cheesemonger sells over a hundred Spanish varieties, as well as *ibérico* ham. Come here for *manchego* or a whole ham. You can complete your shopping at the *Ferretería* (hardware shop) opposite, which has all the utensils you need to slice ham properly.

Alonso Martínez – the business district

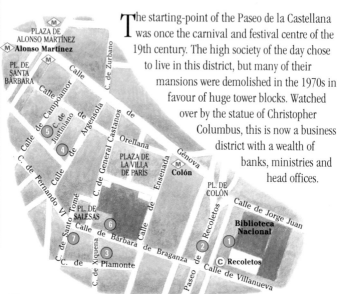

PLAZA DE ALONSO MARTÍNEZ
Ⓜ **Alonso Martínez**

PL. DE SANTA BÁRBARA

Calle

C. de Zurbano

Calle

Calle de Campoamor

C. de Justiniano

C. de Argensola

de

de

Orellana

PLAZA DE LA VILLA DE PARÍS

de General Castaños

Génova

Ⓜ **Colón**

C. de Fernando VI

C. de Santo Tomé

PL. DE SALESAS

Calle

de

Bárbara

de

Ensenada

de

Braganza

PL. DE COLÓN

Calle de Jorge Juan

Biblioteca Nacional

Paseo

de

Recoletos

Ⓒ **Recoletos**

Calle de Villanueva

C. de Xiquena

C. de Piamonte

The starting-point of the Paseo de la Castellana was once the carnival and festival centre of the 19th century. The high society of the day chose to live in this district, but many of their mansions were demolished in the 1970s in favour of huge tower blocks. Watched over by the statue of Christopher Columbus, this is now a business district with a wealth of banks, ministries and head offices.

❶ Biblioteca Nacional★★
Paseo de Recoletos, 20
☎ **91 580 77 59**
Tue.-Sat. 10am-9pm,
Sun. 10am-2pm
Entry free.

With its eleven million volumes, this is the largest building erected in the reign of Isabel II. Inside, the Library makes remarkably good use of an up-to-date interactive system, with the computerised multimedia area forming a striking contrast with the magnificent old book collection, which contains early hand-printed volumes, Charles VIII's book of hours, manuscripts and engravings. You can also learn about the history of writing, printing and various techniques of reproduction.

❷ El Espejo★★★
Paseo de Recoletos, 31
Every day 10-1am.

This restaurant may look as if it dates from the 19th century, but it was actually built in the 1980s. The decoration, with large mirrors and *Modernista* style, is quite superb. Take advantage

of El Espejo's two annexes –
a summer terrace and,
just opposite, the *pabellón*,
its wide-windowed winter
terrace. The tapas are
delicious here. It's ideal
for a quick bite to eat or a
more formal (but also more
expensive) lunch.

❸ Expresion Negra★
Calle Piamonte, 15
☎ 91 319 95 27
Mon.-Sat. 11am-2pm,
5-8pm.

This shop sponsoring African
art doesn't just content itself
with exhibiting artists' works,
it also employs craftsmen to
make things from recycled
objects, including CD and
cassette storage boxes, and
cars. The mixture of genres
is a real success.

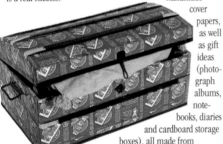

❹ Premillennium★
Calle Argensola, 5
☎ 91 308 40 96
Mon.-Sat. 10am-8.30pm.

With its plastic and kitsch
merchandise, Premillennium
is a gentle reminder of the
1970s. The accent here is
on originality, humour and
bright colours. You'll find an
amusing variety of inflatable
furniture and fluorescent
wallets, along with objects
made of cardboard and
fluffy toys.

❺ De Papel★
Calle Justiniano, 7
☎ 91 319 44 18
Mon.-Fri. 10am-2.30pm,
4.30pm-2am, Sat. 10am-
2.30pm.

This shop sells all kinds of
paper products – recycled
paper, writing paper with
amazing designs and
handmade
cover
papers,
as well
as gift
ideas
(photo-
graph
albums,
note-
books, diaries
and cardboard storage
boxes), all made from
different types of paper.

❻ El Gato Persa★
Calle Barbara de
Braganza, 10
☎ 91 319 31 48
Tea room: 5-8pm
Restaurant: 9pm-1am.

Tea rooms are a rare sight
in Madrid, which makes this
one all the more special.
It has a cosy decor, with
comfortable sofas and wood
panelling, and baroque
music playing softly in the
background. All you have to
do is choose your favourite
tea from the vast variety on
offer, and make your choice
of the delicious tarts and
pastries. In the evening,
El Gato Persa becomes a
restaurant.

❼ EL MENTIDERO DE LA VILLA★★
Calle Santo Tomé, 6
☎ 91 308 12 85
Every day except Sat.
lunchtime, Sun. and
holidays, 1.30-4pm,
9pm-midnight.

Set foot inside this
delightful restaurant
and you'll discover a decor
unlike any other in
Madrid, with *trompe-l'œil*
paintings, wooden horses
separating the different
areas and period furniture.
It serves Franco-Spanish
cuisine combining
traditional and modern
sauces, all washed down
with good local wines.
For a moderate price
(around €12), the menu
is innovative and creative.

Chueca, the traditional to the avant-garde

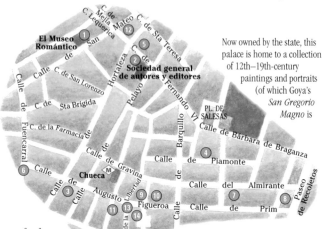

Now owned by the state, this palace is home to a collection of 12th–19th-century paintings and portraits (of which Goya's *San Gregorio Magno* is representative). The twenty-five rooms mainly house paintings of the Romantic period, as well as furniture, ceramics and musical instruments. You should make a point of seeing the piano made by the House of Pleyel for Isabel II and, on a

Not far from the historic city centre, Chueca seems to have two faces. Traditional shops stand side-by-side with the latest trendy boutiques in narrow streets overlooked by *cristaleras*. These balcony windows, typical in Madrid, are maintained and preserved as part of the city's heritage. The surrounding area has recently become the favourite haunt of the gay community. Tradition rubs shoulders with the modern world in the greatest possible harmony.

❶ El Museo Romantico★★

Calle San Mateo,13
☎ **91 448 10 71**
Every day except Mon.
9am-3pm, Sun. and holidays
10am-2pm, closed Aug.
Entry charge except Sun.

note of historical interest, the colour lithographs of *corridas* provide a good insight into bullfighting in times gone by.

❷ Sociedad General de Autores y Editores★★
Calle Fernando VI, 4.

This building, which is one of a kind, is a good example of the early 20th-century *Modernista* movement. It was designed by the architect José Grases Riera. The spiral

central staircase is very beautiful, but the interior of the building is only open to the public on 5 October each year. However, it's worth going just to have a look at the two rounded granite façades.

❸ Shoes that fit like a glove★★

Go along to Calle Figueroa where shoes and accessories sell for amazing prices the whole length of the street. Most of the designs are *muestrarios* – last year's collections. They vary

from the eccentric to the very traditional, but there's just one problem – they often come in only one size – 36 for women (UK 4) and 40 for men (UK 8). If you've got small feet you'll be in seventh heaven but you can always find something a little larger among the current designs.

❹ The traditional shops that are a dying breed★

The *churrería* at Calle Piamonte, 29, is well worth a visit. The owner fries the doughnuts in a huge pan over a wood-burning stove. His wife then sells these delicious *churros* out of wicker baskets in the streets and bars, where they are a favourite with the *Madrileños* for breakfast.

Not far from the *churreria*, at Calle Figueroa, 31, you'll see a shop with its window filled with crisps. They're very tasty and are sold by the weight. This is a good opportunity to try some *kikos*, which are small grains of maize, grilled and salted.

❺ La Duquesa★★
Calle Fernando VI, 2
☎ **91 308 02 31**
Tue.-Sun. 9am-2pm, 5-8pm.

La Duquesa is one of the oldest and best patisseries in Madrid. It looks beautiful on the outside and smells delicious on the inside. Here they make all the specialities of the city according to the season – *polvorones*, *mazapán*, *roscon* and *anguila* at Christmas and *torrijas* and eggs at Easter.

turn of the 20th century. The terrace is still a very tempting place to settle down to read the morning newspaper in peace.

⑨ Casa Santander★★
Calle Figueroa, 25
☎ **91 522 49 10**
Mon.-Fri. 1-4pm,
8.30pm-midnight,
Sat. 8.30pm-midnight.

⑥ Centro Comercial★
Calle Fuencarral, 45
Mon.-Sat. 10am-9pm.

With its breathtaking array of shops selling clothes and accessories, and its original interior design, this shopping centre attracts a very trendy clientèle. If you go down to the basement (open 10-2am), you'll find an internet café, a relaxation room and an auditorium which hosts a varied programme of films, plays and live dance performances.

⑦ LA TIERRA★★
Calle Almirante, 28
☎ **91 521 21 34**
Mon.-Fri. 9.30am-1.30pm,
5-8pm, Sat. 9.30am-
1.30pm.

La Tierra is a little like a popular art gallery. You'll find a range of traditional ceramics with green, blue and white patterns here, as well as some very fine azulejo tiles at tempting prices, so it's an ideal place to bear in mind if you're searching for an unusual gift. The friendly staff will even take the time to explain where the articles come from.

⑧ Café Gijon★★
Paseo de Recoletos, 21
☎ **91 521 54 25**
Every day 10-1am.

Built entirely of wood, this *Modernista*-style café which opened in 1888, is famous for the literary and political discussions that took place here between members of Madrid's café society at the

Casa Santander is an authentic kind of place without any airs or graces and is known for its simplicity and conviviality as well as the quality of the tapas, so make sure you try some. If you stand at the bar, you'll soon make the acquaintance of the regulars and may even fall into conversation with them.

hanging from the shop fronts, as well as fruit such as *chimoyas*, which taste a little like pears, and *chapatas*, the long loaves peculiar to Madrid.

12 Patrimonio Comunal Olivarero
Calle Lequerica, 1
☎ **91 522 49 10**
Mon.-Fri. 10am-2pm, 5-8pm, Sat. 10am-2pm.

The entire olive oil production of Spain is represented in this shop, which is devoted, not to say dedicated, to olive oil. However, as with wines, no two oils are exactly alike. Ask an assistant for advice and you'll be offered some very attractive bottles to take back as presents, as well as oils in metal containers that travel better.

A GOURMET EVENING

10 La Tienda de Vinos
Calle Figueroa, 35
Mon.-Fri. 1-4pm, 8.30pm-midnight, Sat. 8.30pm-midnight.

This restaurant has been nicknamed 'el communista' for so long that no-one can remember why. Although renowned for its cuisine, it's still quite unpretentious and you'll be able to enjoy a tasty meal here for a very reasonable price. The atmosphere, of course, comes as a bonus.

11 San Anton covered market*
On the corner of Calle Figueroa and Calle Libertad
Mon.-Fri. 9am-2pm, 5-8pm.

If you want to familiarise yourself with the local produce, pay a visit to this covered market. As you mingle with the locals, you'll discover all kinds of hams and sausages

13 Bocaito
Calle Libertad, 6
☎ **91 532 12 19**
Mon.-Fri. 1-4pm, 8.30pm-midnight, Sat. 8.30-midnight.

The *Madrileños* aren't mistaken – these really are the best tapas in the neighbourhood. The place is always full at aperitif time. It's a great place to meet people.

14 La Carmencita
Calle Libertad, 16
☎ **91 531 66 12**
Mon.-Fri. 1-4pm, 9pm-midnight, Sat. 8.30pm-midnight.

Come here for a meal before setting out on a bar crawl. The little rooms lined with azulejo tiles make an intimate setting for the delicious dishes. It's definitely a good way to start the evening.

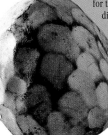

Malasaña, a hotbed of resistance

The name 'Plaza del Dos de Mayo' commemorates the fierce resistance put up by the people of Madrid against the forces of Napoleon. It forms the heart of an ageing, working-class district that 'always appears ailing but never dies'. The statue in the centre of the square depicts two men swearing an oath of resistance against the French invaders. In recent years, Malasaña has shown that it's still a symbol of popular action.

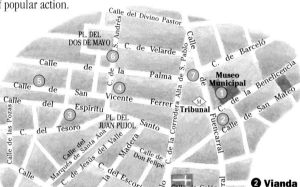

❷ Vianda Asturiana★

Calle Fuencarral, 47
☎ 91 523 18 95
Mon.-Fri.
10am-2pm, 5-8pm,
Sat. 10am-2pm.

There's nothing quite like pausing for some gourmet treats. All the products on sale here come from the north of the country, Cantabria, Galicia and Asturias. With oil, vinegar, herb tea, honey, charcuterie, cheese and a good selection of wines on offer, there's plenty to make your mouth water. It's a good place to start in this ultra-trendy street.

❶ Museo Municipal★

Calle Fuencarral, 78
☎ 91 588 86 72
Tue.-Fri. 9.30am-8pm,
Sat.-Sun. 10am-2pm
Entry charge.

If you're keen to learn about the history of Madrid, you'll find this museum housed in the city's former hospice particularly interesting.

You can follow the city's urban and social development from its foundation to the present day. Don't miss *La Alegoria de la Villa de Madrid* by Goya and the model of Plaza de Toros at the time of its construction.

❸ Ama Records
Calle Espíritu Santo, 25
☎ **91 521 34 89**
Mon.-Fri. 11am-2pm,
5-9pm.

This record shop sells all the latest electronic dance music on CD or vinyl, including house, jungle, hip hop, acid and many more. If you feel like dancing, the assistant will be delighted to let you have the addresses of some of the best clubs.

❹ Corner of Calle San Vicente Ferrer and Calle San Andrés★

Make sure you take a look at this former chemist's shop if you are passing. It's covered in azulejo tile designs extolling the merits of such miracle cures as cough syrup and indigestion tablets and is both unusual and entertaining.

❺ Café Manuela★★
Calle San Vicente Ferrer, 9
☎ **91 531 70 37**
Every day 3.30pm-3am.

This welcoming café with patinated walls is one of the best-known in the city. People come here for a drink, to chat

with friends or simply to read the newspaper. The cocktails are delicious, especially the *caipirinia*. They host poetry readings and *tertulias* which take place several times a month at around 8.30pm. Ask at the bar if you'd like to know more details.

❻ El 2De★
Calle San Andrés, 25
Mon.-Sat. 4pm-1am.

With its ceiling fans and round marble-topped tables, this very old bistro, which opens onto Plaza del Dos de Mayo, still looks the same as it did years ago. It's the perfect place to start off a lively evening frequenting some of the district's fashionable bars.

❼ Calle Fuencarral★
A large number of clothes shops, such as *Mala Postura* and *No Comment*, have opened in this street where you'll also find trendy 1970s-style merchandise on offer. If you really want to be *a la ultima* (in the latest fashion), various trendy accessories as well as piercing and tattoos are at your disposal.

❽ El Horno de San Onofre★★
Calle San Onofre, 3
☎ **91 532 90 60**
Mon.-Sun. 9am-8pm.

The sight and aroma of this old-fashioned patisserie will be enough to make you want to go inside. Besides the traditional cakes at Christmas time, they make *turrón*, *polvorones*, *mazapanes* and *roscones de reyes* that are rumoured to be the best in Madrid, so if you've got a sweet tooth, make straight for this shop.

❾ Iglesia de San Placido★
Calle San Roque, 9
☎ **91 531 79 99**
Mon.-Fri. 10am-noon,
5-6pm, Sat. 5-6pm,
Sun. 11am-noon, 5-6pm.

This delightful Baroque church was built in the 17th century. You must go in and see the altarpiece framing a marvellous depiction of the Annunciation painted by Claudio Coello in 1668.

The residential district of Rubén Darío

Built in the second half of the 19th century, the charming district of Rubén Darío was once a magnet for aristocrats and businessmen. Now occupied by diplomatic services, offices and smart flats, it lacks a real architectural unity, but is still worth visiting for its rich historical past.

(map: showing Calle de María de Molina, Hoyos, Calle de López, Paseo, Calle del General Oráa, Museo Lázaro Galdiano ①, ②, C. de Claudio Coello, Calle de Diego, C. de León, Museo Sorolla ④, Zurbano, Angel, Miguel, Paseo del General Martínez Campos, GLORIETA DE EMILIO CASTELAR, Calle, Calvo ⑤, ⑦, Rafael ⑥, C. de, de, Fortuny, la Castellana, Juan Bravo ③, GLORIETA DE RUBÉN DARÍO, Paseo de Eduardo Dato, C. de Almagro, Rubén Darío (M), Calle de Jenner)

❶ Museo Lázaro Galdiano★★

Calle Serrano, 122
☎ **91 561 60 84**
Tue.-Sun. 10am-2pm
Entry charge except Sat.

The Museo Lázaro Galdiano is an excellent complement to the Prado for those who want to refine their knowledge of art history. This sumptuous mansion once belonged to businessman Jose Lazaro Galdiano. Inside, you can admire the rich collection that he bequeathed to the nation on his death. The tour starts on the ground floor with Italian bronzes and continues with paintings representing the European schools of the period. There are also beautiful Limoges enamels, inlaid furniture, small sculptures and a collection of fob watches on display.

❷ José Luis★

Calle Serrano, 89-91
☎ **91 563 09 58**
Every day 8-1am.

José Luis's tapas are renowned throughout Madrid. The *tortilla* is said to be the best in the city and the *pinchos* (especially the crab *pincho*) will make your mouth water. The five restaurants that José

Luis Solaguren has opened in Madrid are never empty, so do make a point of trying one of them.

❸ La Galería ABC★★
Calle Serrano, 61
Mon.-Sat. 10am-9pm.

All kinds of shops have been brought together in this mini-shopping centre. You'll find a gallery of boutiques specialising in interior design, clothes (including a branch of Zara – see page 88), shoes and children's toys, as well as a cafeteria. If you like shopping, this place has a good selection of the type of things Madrid has to offer.

❹ Museo Sorolla★★
Paseo General Martínez Campos, 37
☎ 91 310 17 31
Tue.-Sat. 10am-3pm, Sun. and holidays 10am-2pm
Entry charge.

The Impressionist painter Joaquin Sorolla Bastida (1863-1923) lived and worked here. His works (notes, paintings, drawings and sculptures) are displayed over three floors, along with his own furniture which has been preserved. Surrounded by three gardens decorated with azulejo tiles and little fountains that give it an Andalusian air, the museum is quite charming.

❺ Fortuny
Calle Fortuny 34
☎ 91 319 05 88
Every day 1pm-4am.

In the setting of a former palace, Fortuny is currently very much in vogue. The first two floors have been turned into a bar, while the top floor now houses a restaurant. The most pleasant spot in the warmer months is the terrace-garden. If you're looking for a really lively atmosphere, don't come before 2am.

❻ Piedra★★
Calle Zurbano, 43
☎ 91 319 89 49
Mon.-Fri. 10am-2pm, 5-8pm,
Sat. 10.30am-2pm.

This kind of ethnic jewellery shop is very rare in Madrid. Here you'll find original antique and contemporary jewellery originating from Central Asia and India, made from gold or silver set with precious and semi-precious stones. Some of the delicate silver bracelets are simply stunning.

❼ EL BOULEVARD★★
Paseo de la Castellana, 37
☎ 91 808 52 58
15 May-30 Sep., every day 9am-5pm.

In fine weather, the city's inhabitants head for the streets. Until late at night, they stroll from terrace to terrace, taking up much of the Paseo de la Castellana and the Paseo de Recoletos. El Boulevard is *the* most fashionable terrace in Madrid. It's the place to see and be seen, and is at the heart of *Madrileño* nightlife.

Rooms and restaurants
Practicalities

Every year the number of charming hotels in Spain increases. Until now Madrid, unfortunately, has had few of them. The choice has always been between a few luxury hotels and lots of old fashioned ones, but this is all changing as many are being bought up by larger hotel chains and tastefully renovated.

CHOOSING A HOTEL

In Spain, a hotel can mean a guest house, cheap family accommodation, an inexpensive one to three-star *bostál* or a one to five-star hotel. Three, four and five star categories include a telephone, television, en-suite bathroom and air conditioning, which is essential in the hot summer months. Some hotels, such as the Serrano have no official star rating but are nevertheless first class. The prices shown on the following pages generally don't include breakfast or VAT (at 7%). Almost all hotels offer special weekend reductions of between 9% and 50%. Check before you go as the reductions aren't always available.

MAKING A RESERVATION

If you want to stay at a particular hotel in the high season (Sept.–Oct., Feb.–Mar. and May–Jun.), it's a good idea to book well in advance. Three-star hotels are packed during exhibitions and fiestas (and there are plenty of them in Madrid). All you have to do to book is to send a fax or email the hotel. In return, you'll be asked to pay a deposit by credit card or eurocheque. You can also book easily and conveniently on the internet. Try a booking service such as www.octopustravel.com where you'll be able to compare prices and facilities.

RESTAURANTS

There's something to suit all tastes and budgets. The traditional taverns will allow you to sample the delights of Madrid cuisine, including *cordero asado* (grilled lamb), *cochinillo* (suckling pig), *chuletas de cordero* (lamb chops) and many other delicious dishes. They're usually to be found in the historic centre of Madrid. Various regional cuisines, and Basque cuisine in particular, are also on offer. As in any other self-respecting capital, it's important not to overlook the fashionable restaurants where people go to see and be seen. Lastly, Asian restaurants, though few and far between, are well worth a visit.

SPANISH MEALTIMES

It's a well-known fact that the Spanish have their own ideas when it comes to mealtimes. Breakfast is eaten early, but you often see workers popping down to the corner bar for a second breakfast, usually consisting of coffee or hot chocolate and *churros* (long, thin doughnuts), *croisán a la plancha* (a croissant cut in half and toasted), *tostada* (white toast) or just a *pincho* (a small portion of tapas). Few Spaniards have lunch before

2pm – it's more usual to have it around 2.30 or even 3pm. Restaurants usually open around 1.30pm, but if you go there at that time you'll find the place empty and you'll have to wait at least half an hour before anyone else arrives. If you're famished, you can always pop into a tapas bar, some of which are open all day long. Although some restaurants open as early as 8.30pm in the evening, most Spaniards don't arrive much before 10pm. It's up to you whether you want to have the place to yourself. If not, you can wait and do as the Spanish do, in other words start by having an aperitif in a tapas bar before going on to dine. Generally speaking, it's essential to book a table in most restaurants, especially at the weekend.

VAT AND TIPS

Some restaurants include VAT (at 7%) in their prices, others don't. Remember to check if you don't want to get a shock. As a rule, service is included in the bill, but it's traditional to leave around 5% of the total.

TERRACES

From early June, the tables and chairs come out and outdoor terraces open up everywhere, especially on the Paseo del Prado, Paseo de Recoletos and Paseo de la Castellana. They're open all day long until late at night and the people of Madrid flock to them in droves. The best-known, the Boulevard (see page 69), is still packed at around 1am. Most terraces are only open from June to September, however.

QUICK GUIDE TO COFFEE

If you want to start the day in the right way, or avoid ending up with a milky coffee when you like it strong and black, read the following carefully.

Café solo:
very strong, black coffee.

Café americano:
large cup of not-so-strong coffee.

Café cortado:
coffee with a dash of milk.

Café con leche:
white coffee.

Café con hielo:
iced coffee (very popular in summer).

PRICES

It's obviously quite possible to find a very cheap restaurant, especially at lunchtime (with set meal for around €6).

However, the good restaurants, and the so-called trendy ones, are usually quite expensive. Expect to pay at least €25 per person for a meal, including wine.

HOTELS

Lopez de Hoyos

Hotel Emperatriz★★★★

Calle Lopez de Hoyos, 4
☎ 91 563 80 88
🖷 91 563 98 04
Email: comercial@hotel-emperatiz.com
Around €165, weekend rate 33% discount.

A modern hotel in a quiet, airy location near Salamanca. It boasts fine parquet flooring and the very latest wooden furniture. Try to get one of the rooms with a terrace.

Rubén Darío

Santo Mauro Hotel★★★★★

Calle Zurbano, 36
☎ 91 319 69 00
🖷 91 308 54 77
Email santo-mauro@itelco.es
Around €230.

Once the townhouse owned by the dukes of Santo Mauro, this luxury hotel has 26 rooms with an ultramodern decor and a swimming pool in the vaulted basement. The library has been turned into a gourmet restaurant, the Belagua, whose garden and terrace are an extremely pleasant place to dine out in summer.

Hotel Orfila★★★★★

Calle Orfila, 6
☎ 91 702 77 70
🖷 91 702 77 72
Email hotelorfila@sei.es
Around €270, weekend rate 15% discount.

This small 19th-century palace was recently converted into a charming luxury hotel. Its 28 rooms and 4 suites are tastefully decorated and the terrace is modest but pleasant.

Hotel Tryp Escultor★★★★

Calle Miguel Angel, 3
☎ 91 310 42 03
🖷 91 319 25 84
Around €160, weekend rate 45% discount.

Overlooking the Glorieta Rubén Darío, this hotel's façade is a little disappointing. However, the interior is a great success. Many of the 85 spacious rooms have private sitting rooms, and the weekend rates are especially attractive.

Chueca

Hotel Mónaco★★

Calle Barbieri, 5
☎ 91 522 46 30
🖷 91 521 16 01
Around €42.

This is a haven of peace in a lively district. Housed in a former brothel, the 34 sizeable rooms with parquet flooring, large windows, air conditioning and televisions, have an air of decadence. It's an ideal location for those who like shopping and going out in the evening, and offers very good value for money

Hostál Greco★★

Calle Infantas, 3
☎ 91 522 46 32
🖷 91 523 23 61
Around €60.

Also a former brothel, once frequented by members of high society, the Hostál Greco still displays a few reminders of its past, including mirrors and frescoes of women in various

stages of undress. Each bedroom on the first floor has its own individual character. It's good value, original and in an excellent location.

Alonso Martínez

Hotel NH Embajada★★★

Calle Santa Engracia, 5
☎ 91 594 02 13
☎ 91 447 33 12
Email www.nh-hoteles.es
Around €135, weekend rate
8% discount.

A stone's throw from Plaza Alonso Martínez and Chueca, this hotel has 101 modern, functional rooms. The decor, with light wooden walls and modern paintings is a great success, and the façade is very inviting.

Salamanca

Hotel Husa Serrano Royal★★★★

Calle de Marqués de Villamejor, 8
☎ 91 576 96 26
☎ 91 575 33 07
Email hparis@eniac.es
Around €165.

Hotel Wellington★★★★★

Calle Velázquez, 8
☎ 91 575 44 00 or
91 575 52 00
☎ 91 576 41 64
Email wellin@genio.infor.es
Around €220, weekend rate
25% discount.

This large, luxury hotel is well situated close to the Parque del Retiro. You may be lucky

Next door to the Galeria ABC stands one of the smallest and best hotels in Madrid. It has large, comfortable rooms and a very pleasant breakfast room, with furniture covered in white fabric. The weekend rates are very attractive.

enough to come across some of the great names of bullfighting, who come here to dress in their finery before entering the bullring. The rooms are fairly spacious and the hotel has a swimming pool, which is rare in Madrid.

NH Sanvy★★★★

Calle Goya, 3
☎ 91 576 08 00
☎ 91 575 24 43
Email www.nh-hoteles.es
Around €135, weekend rate
8% discount.

This hotel overlooks Plaza Colón at the intersection of the Salamanca, Alonso Martínez and Chueca districts. Take no notice of the somewhat uninviting façade. The hotel is part of the NH chain and is decorated in a similar style to the rest.

Hotel Tryp Fenix★★★★

Calle Hermosilla, 2
☎ 91 431 67 00
☎ 91 575 16 94
Email hotel@tryp.es
Weekend rate €95.

A few years ago, this very fine hotel with over 200 rooms was taken over by the Spanish chain, Tryp. They modernised it while leaving the 50s decor of the lounges, with their abundance of marble, untouched. The rooms are both spacious and comfortable and the hotel is bustling and well situated for a visit to the city.

Hotel NH Lagasca★★★

Calle Lagasca, 64
☎ 91 575 46 06
☎ 91 575 16 94
Email www.nh-hoteles.es
NH chain reservation centre
902 115 116
Around €135, weekend rate
9% discount.

With 100 rooms decorated in a modern, functional style, this hotel is located in the heart of the Salamanca district. If you want to do some shopping, you couldn't find a better place to stay.

Gran Hotel Velázquez★★★★

Calle Velázquez, 62
☎ 91 575 28 00
✆ 91 577 51 31
Email jcrodri@cestel.es
Around €110, weekend rate 30% discount.

An old-fashioned hotel in the heart of Salamanca, close to the Fundación Juan March. The decor is a little elaborate, but the atmosphere has a real Spanish charm. The rooms are vast but slightly outmoded.

Plaza Santa Ana

BW Hotel Cortezo★★★

Calle Doctor Cortezo, 3
☎ 91 369 01 01
✆ 91 369 37 74
Around €85.

In a quiet spot, near the lively Plaza Santa Ana, this hotel is part of the Best Western chain, a guarantee of value for money. The rooms are simple and clean, furnished with reproduction antique furniture.

Gran Hotel Tryp Reina Victoria★★★★

Plaza Santa Ana, 14
☎ 91 531 45 00
✆ 91 522 03 07
Around €157, rates vary according to season.

This marvellously-situated hotel, once visited by Ernest Hemingway, was built on the site of the former palace belonging to the counts of Teba. It's one of the meeting-places of the world of bullfighting. If you come during a *corrida*, you may pass a *torero* dressed for the bullring with his *cuadrilla* (the group of *picadors* and *bandilleros* who assist him). The 201 rooms are modern and comfortable.

Green Prado★★★

Calle Prado, 11
☎ 93 369 02 34
✆ 91 429 28 29
Email prado@green-hoteles.com
Around €120, weekend rate 25% discount.

This little hotel, in the neighbourhood of Puerta del Sol, Plaza Mayor and the Santa Ana district, has 50 ultramodern rooms that have just been renovated. It's strategically located for visiting the city.

Palacio Real

Hotel Tryp Ambassador★★★★

Cuesta de Santo Domingo, 5 and 7
☎ 91 541 67 00
✆ 91 559 10 40
Email hotel@tryp.es
Around €157, weekend rate 44% discount.

Housed in the former palace of the dukes of Granada de Ega, this very fine hotel stands in an interesting position between the Palacio Real and Teatro Real. Great care has been taken over the interior decoration, with antique furniture and lush plants. The winter garden has been turned into a restaurant.

Hotel Sofitel★★★★

Plaza de España
☎ 91 541 98 80
✆ 91 542 57 36
Email sofitelpza@dirac.es
Around €217, weekend rate 47% discount.

In the vicinity of the Palacio Real, Plaza de Oriente and Museo Cerralbo, this hotel has 96 rooms (and one suite). It has been totally renovated, guaranteeing comfort as well as a good location.

Puerta del Sol

Hotel BW Arosa★★★★

Calle de la Salud, 21
☎ 91 532 16 00
✆ 91 531 31 27
Around €120

Four beautiful chandeliers in the entrance hall set the tone for this hotel, which was a former inn. The reception is on the second floor and the whole place has

been entirely renovated by the Best Western chain. The rooms have good soundproofing, which is a definite asset in this district.

Hotel Santo Domingo★★★★

Plaza de Santo Domingo, 13
☎ 91 547 98 00
✆ 91 547 59 95

Email sdomingo@stnet.es
Around €148, weekend rate 25% discount.

With 25 well-decorated rooms and light, spacious lounges with fine furniture and old paintings, this is a charming place well worth remembering.

Hotel Liabeny★★★★

Calle Salud, 3
☎ 91 531 90 00
✆ 91 532 74 21

Email liabeny@apunte.es
Around €120, weekend rate 25% discount.

A large, slightly old-fashioned hotel, close to the Puerta del Sol. The wood panelling and leather armchairs give the lounge a true Spanish feel. The rooms are decorated in a similar style.

Hotel Gaudi★★★★

Gran Vía, 9
☎ 91 531 22 22
✆ 91 531 54 69
Around €145.

People come to this hotel for its central location and comfortable, modern rooms. It's the choice of many businessmen because of its proximity to the head offices of many of the larger companies, especially the banks. After a tiring day walking and sightseeing, take advantage of the gymnasium and sauna and let your cares and worries float away.

La Residencia de El Viso★★★

Calle Nervión, 8
☎ 91 564 03 70
✆ 91 564 19 65
Around €115.

This modern hotel has its own charm. Although it's very close to the historic centre, it enjoys a privileged location in a peaceful, airy district. The rooms are quiet and the terrace is a pleasant place to rest after a day's sightseeing in the city centre. It's recommended if you want to escape the hustle and bustle. There are no weekend rates.

Ritz★★★★★

Plaza de la Lealtad, 5
☎ 91 701 67 67
✆ 91 701 67 76
Email www.ritz.es
Around €635.

If you want a special night to remember, this is the place to come. Opened in 1910 as a hotel for the aristocracy, the Ritz offers the height of luxury, elegance and the kind of comfort you can't find elsewhere, as well as their renowned impeccable service. With a terrace and magnificent garden, it's even more pleasant in summer.

RESTAURANTS

República Argentina

No-Do

Calle Velázquez, 150
☎ 91 564 40 44
Every day 1.30-4pm, 9pm-midnight
Around €24.

With its modern, dark wood decor and calm atmosphere, this is currently the in-place. It's a good place for an introduction to Mediterranean-Japanese cuisine. If you're not sure what to order, try the *tataki de atún*, (tuna) which is quite delicious. A word of advice – it's quieter upstairs.

Casa Benigna

Calle Benigno Soto, 9
☎ 91 413 33 58
Every day 1.30-4pm, 9-11pm
Around €36.

With a decor in shades of blue and white, you could easily imagine yourself in a Mediterranean villa here. The owner takes the time to explain the menu and the inventive cuisine is based on top-quality produce. Come and enjoy a real gourmet meal in a pleasant setting. Casa Benigna is definitely one of our favourites.

Salamanca

El Amparo

Calle Puigcerdá, 8
☎ 91 431 64 56
Mon.-Fri. 1.30-3.30pm, 9.30-11.30pm.
Around €78.

One of the finest restaurants in Madrid, with a veritable feast of gourmet delicacies created by head chef Martín Berasategui.

Try the *milhojas de manzana ácida con pescado ahumado y foie gras* (mille-feuille of smoked fish with apple and foie gras) or the *lomos de merluza en salsa verde con almejas* (hake in green sauce with clams).

Bomarzo

Calle Jorge Juan, 16
☎ 91 431 58 40
Mon.-Fri. 2-5pm, 9pm-1am, Sat. 9pm-1am
Around €21.

This restaurant offers more in terms of atmosphere than cuisine, since the latter is decidedly international. With dark blue walls, candles and mirrors everywhere, the decor has a definite baroque theme. The restaurant, which attracts a young, trendy crowd, is on the first floor and is warm and friendly.

When you come back down after dinner, you can enjoy a drink or two at the bar, if you're not too full of course!

Viridiana

Calle Juan de Mena, 14
☎ 91 523 44 78
Mon.-Sat. 1.30-4pm, 9pm-midnight, closed Aug.
Gourmet set meal €60.

The owner, Abraham García, is both a cinema-lover and one of the best cooks in Madrid. He combines his two passions by decorating his restaurant with photos from Buñuel films and serving the most inventive cuisine in the city. On top of all this, his cellar contains over 500 fine wines from all over the world.

El Alkalde

Calle Jorge Juan, 10
☎ 91 576 33 59
Every day 1-5pm, 7.30pm-midnight
Around €33.

Serving all the great classics of Basque cuisine, El Alkalde is frequented by regulars and was at the height of its popularity in the 1980s. You can order tapas at the bar on the ground floor, while the restaurant proper is in the basement. Try a *cola de merluza rellena* (stuffed tail of hake)– it's quite delicious.

Thai Gardens

Calle Jorge Juan, 5
☎ 91 577 88 84
Mon.-Sun. 2-4pm,
9pm-midnight
Gourmet set meal €25.

Although this restaurant isn't very typical of Madrid the beauty of the setting and the quality of the Thai cuisine make it a place not to be missed. After making your way down a corridor, you'll be pleasantly surprised by the tropical plants of the winter garden, the wooden furniture and the pretty fountain. Served by polite waitresses, you'll think you've arrived on a different continent.

Irocco

Calle Velázquez, 18
☎ 91 431 73 81
Mon.-Sat. 2-4pm,
9.30pm-midnight,
Sun. 2.30-4.30pm, 9-11pm
Around €30.

With almond green walls, designer furniture and soft lighting, this restaurant has a very welcoming atmosphere.

If you visit Madrid in the summer, this is definitely the place to come It's a real pleasure to have dinner on the terrace on very hot days. Brunch is served every Sunday from 2.30pm onwards.

Casa Manolo

Calle Orellana, 17
☎ 91 319 23 92
Mon.-Fri. 1-4pm
Set meal €11.

You won't enough time to get to know this typical restaurant properly if you're only here for a weekend. It's an old neighbourhood bistro that's packed every lunchtime. The chef serves good, traditional cuisine such as *cordero a la pastora* (lamb) and *judías con perdiz* (beans with partridge). The only problem is that you'll need a siesta after your meal!

Sinfonia Italiana di Sapori e Profumi

Calle Fernando El Santo, 25
☎ 91 308 12 96
Mon.-Sat. 10-2am
Around 5,500 ptas.

This tiny restaurant has just five tables for two people. The quiet background music and display of olive oils and other Italian produce give it a cosy feel. The regulars are fans of 'slow food', in other words, the best quality produce cooked to order. It means you'll have to wait for your risotto, but all the dishes are absolutely delicious and the menu changes frequently. If you want to have lunch, arrive at about 2.30pm, and if you don't want to spend the entire afternoon here, order the same main course as your dining partner.

La Gastroteca de Stéphane y Arturo

Plaza de Chueca, 8
☎ 91 532 25 64
Mon.-Fri. 2-3.30pm, 9-11pm,
Sat. 9-11pm, closed Aug.
Around €36.

A place that's one of a kind. Opened 12 years ago by a French architect, writer and painter, this unusual bistro, with a pink and black decor, serves highly creative cuisine. The black olive sorbet is just one of a number of unusual dishes you can find on the menu.

Salvador

Calle Barbieri, 12
☎ **91 521 45 24 or**
91 531 51 00
Mon.-Sat. 1.30-4pm,
9-11.30pm
Around €25.

Nothing has changed much in this place since it opened in 1941. If you're a fan of bullfighting, you'll feel at home here – the walls are covered with photos, posters and paintings, all relating to Spain's traditional sport. The house specialities are bull's tail and *merluza rebozada* (hake in breadcrumbs). It has a traditional Spanish setting, with a livelier atmosphere at lunchtime than in the evening.

Palacio Real

Entre Suspiro y Suspiro

Calle Caños del Peral, 3
☎ **91 542 06.44**
Mon.-Fri. 2-4pm,
9-11.30pm,
Sat. 9-11.30pm
Around €27.

Mexican cuisine as opposed to Tex-Mex. Tasty, traditional, dishes that you may not have tried before, to savour surrounded by a fine collection of tequila bottles and paintings by Mexican artists. Start with *ceviche de gambas* (prawns) or *revuelto de cuitlacoche* (scrambled eggs) followed by *solomillo al mole* (ground sirloin).

La Ópera de Madrid

Calle Amnistía, 5
☎ **91 559 50 92**
Mon.-Fri. 1.30-4pm,
9-11.30pm, Sat. 9-11.30pm
Around €27.

A slightly old-fashioned restaurant with a warm, intimate

atmosphere, decorated with parquet flooring, wood panelling, paintings, engravings and chandeliers shedding a soft glow. A short walk from the Teatro Real, the audience comes here after the performance to savour the Mediterranean cuisine.

Vaca Argentina

Calle Bailén, 20
☎ **91 365 66 54**
Every day 1-4.30pm,
9pm-12.30am
Around 4,500 ptas.

As the name suggests, the excellent beef served in this restaurant comes straight from Argentina. People come here for the quality of the meat rather than the charming atmosphere, however, if there isn't room, there are five other restaurants belonging to the same chain in Madrid.

is exquisite and the wine waiter offers invaluable advice. Booking essential, jacket required.

Banco de España

Gula Gula

Gran Vía, 1
☎ **91 522 87 64**
Every day 1-4.30pm,
9pm-2am
Around €18.

If you're looking for somewhere lively, this is the place to come. With a breathtaking view from the first floor, you'll find a relaxed atmosphere, colourful decor and disco music. The menu includes a variety of salads followed by a hot dish and, to top it all, a drag show. It's a popular venue for hen nights.

Rubén Darío

Zalacaín

Calle Alvarez de Baena, 4
☎ **91 561 48 40**
Mon.-Fri. 1.30-3.45pm,
9-11.45pm, Sat. 9-11.45pm,
closed Easter week, holidays and Aug.
Gourmet set meal €70.

Probably the best restaurant in Madrid, if not the whole of Spain. Served in the glorious setting of a 19th-century townhouse, the chef Benjamin Urdiain's cuisine

Puerta del Sol

Mad

Calle de Virgén de Peligros, 4
☎ **91 532 62 28**
Mon.-Fri. 2-5pm,
8.30pm-1am
Around €30.

Mad's terrace is very pleasant in the evening, with its lush plants and marvellous view of a beautiful, illuminated church. A mass of candles greet you on your way in. Once inside, the restaurant has the atmosphere of a New

York loft, with grey walls and floors and metal furniture. After a tasty Mediterranean dinner you can enjoy a drink at the bar.

La Látina

Botín

Calle Cuchilleros, 17
☎ 91 365 42 17
Every day 1-4pm,
8pm-midnight
Around €27.

Situated in one of Madrid's older streets, Botín is popular with tourists. Dating from 1725 it's the oldest restaurant in the world, according to the Guinness Book of Records. Ask for *cochinillo asado con patatos* (roast suckling pig), a speciality of Segovia, and try to get a table downstairs.

La Viuda de Vacas

Calle Cava Alta 23
☎ 91 366 58 47
Fri.-Wed. 1-4.30pm,
9pm-midnight, closed Sun.
evening and Thu.
Around €33.

This charming little restaurant, in the heart of a lively district, is housed in an old tavern dating from 1780. There are old azulejo tiles on the walls, wooden tables and a zinc bar, and it's been run by the same family for three generations. It serves excellent everyday cooking that's popular with locals and tourists alike, so don't arrive too late in the evening.

Casa Lucio

Calle Cava Baja, 35
☎ 91 365 32 52
Sun.-Fri. 1-3.45,
9pm-midnight, Sat. 9pm-
midnight, closed Aug.
Around €36.

Casa Lucio is one of the classic Madrid nightspots. People come here to see and be seen, but also to savour the delicious traditional dishes made by a master of the art, Lucio Blazquez. Do try *los callos* (tripe) or *judías con perdiz* (beans with partridge), and ask to be seated in the main room with the old brick vaulted ceiling.

Julián de Tolosa

Calle Cava Baja, 18
☎ 91 365 81 10
Mon.-Sat. 1.30-4pm,
9pm-midnight
Around €36.

If you love good meat, this excellent restaurant, located in a very pleasant setting, is ideal. The chef, Julián de Tolosa, is renowned for cooking the best *chuletones de buey* (ribs of beef) in the city. To start your meal, order the *pimientos del piquillo*, which are particularly delicious. You won't be sorry you came.

Colón

Al Mounia

Calle Recoletos, 5
☎ 91 435 08 28
Tue.-Sat. 1.30-4pm,
9-11.30pm, closed Aug.
and Easter week
Gourmet set meal €30.

When it opened in 1968, Al Mounia was the first restaurant in Madrid to serve Moroccan cuisine. It now has more competition but it's still the best. Comfortably seated in a room decorated with azulejo tiles, you can tuck into tasty couscous or stew, or simply drink mint tea accompanied by some delicious Moroccan pastries.

Alcobendas (northern suburbs)

En Bendeja

La Granja, 104
Polígono Industrial
de Alcobendas
☎ 91 661 21 37

Mon.-Sat. 1-4pm, 9pm-1am,
Sun. 1-4pm
Around €25.

A colourful restaurant housed in an old factory. You'll have to make an effort to get here, since it's impossible to reach by metro, bus or car (unless you don't mind getting lost). You only have one choice – come by taxi. The idea is simple enough – everything you can see in the restaurant is for sale, and the cuisine is good value for money.

DAYTIME CAFÉS AND TEA ROOMS

There are relatively few tea rooms in Madrid. On the other hand, there are many cafés where you can stop for a break over coffee and *churros* in the daytime.

Bilbao

Café Comercial

Glorieta de Bilbao, 7
☎ 91 521 56 55
Every day 7.30-1am.

Since it opened in 1887, this café has never been empty. If what the owners say is true, up to 25,000 people a month pass through this establishment. It's a sign of the times that, besides a large dining room and a terrace for sunny days, there are also computers offering Internet access.

Banco de España

Los Gatos

Calle Jesús, 2
☎ 91 429 30 67
Every day 11-2am.

This bar, decorated with posters and memorabilia connected with bullfighting, has a really welcoming atmosphere. You can either stand at the bar with the locals or find a seat in the small room. If you feel like a bite to eat, try the prawn canapés or Guijuelo charcuterie washed down with a glass of traditional draught beer.

Near Colón

Embassy

Paseo de la Castellana, 12
☎ 91 576 48 77
Every day 9.30-1am.

A tea room with a traditional English decor that's echoed by the muffins and scones on the dessert menu. You can choose from a wide range of teas or plump for a cup of delicious hot chocolate. It's not at all what you'd expect in Madrid.

Underwood Café

Infantas, 32
☎ 91 532 82 67
Every day 4pm-1.30am.

Fans of the popular press will find something to please them here. Old printing plates of original pages dating from the 18th century and a turn-of-the-century radio are reminders that this was once the head office of the first Spanish daily newspaper. The names of the house specialities, such as *Diario de Jerez* (with brandy) and *Monde* (with Benedictine), reflect the original theme of the café. These days, all the national and international papers are available, and so is CNN.

Austrías

Delic

**Calle Costillana de San
Andrés, 14
☎ 91 364 54 50
Every day
9am-mid.,
Fri.-Sat.
until 2am.**

Delic as in
Delicatessen.
The three
little
rooms
opening
onto the lovely Plaza de
la Paja are very simply
decorated. You can eat
here or take away and
they serve breakfast, tea,
full meals as well as
drinks and snacks. The
homemade tarts are highly
recommended.

Huertas

La Esquina del Café

**Calle Huertas, 70
Mon.-Fri. 7.30-2am,
Sat.-Sun. 9-2am.**

Currently very fashionable in
Madrid, coffee is served in
a number of different ways
here. In this small café with
patinated walls, it's served hot
or cold, with or without alcohol,
with vanilla ice cream or with
fresh cream. It could be your
chance to see coffee in a
new light.

La Busca

**Calle Huertas, 74
☎ 91 429 33 52
Sun.-Thu. 9-2am,
Fri.-Sat. 11-3am.**

Connoisseurs should take note,
the coffee here comes from a
whole host of different countries,
including Brazil, Jamaica,

Hawaii, Puerto Rico, and Guate-
mala, and is quite delicious. The
modern decor, with its blue and
yellow painted walls and quiet
little corners, make it an ideal
place to have breakfast. In the
evening, the music gets louder
and cocktails replace the coffee.
As is often the case in the bars of
Madrid, you can have tapas at
any time of day.

Palais Royal

La Madriguera

**Calle Santiago, 3
☎ 91 559 33 45
Tue.-Fri. 9.30am-midnight,
Sat.-Sun. noon-1am.**

Literary cafés such as this one
are fairly new to Madrid. You can
buy a book or read the newspaper while having coffee, to the
sound of classical music playing
in the background. If you're
feeling hungry, you can always
order some tapas. *Tertulias*,
poetry readings and exhibitions
take place monthly on a regular
basis.

Salamanca

Mezzaluna

**Calle Jorge Juan, 50
☎ 91 575 48 80
Every day except Sun.
evening 11.30-1am.**

This pleasant, friendly place with
a Brooklyn-style decor has fine
parquet flooring and cream
walls. Mezzaluna is both a restaurant and a bar, where people
come for a drink at the start of
the evening. Live concerts are
held every Tuesday.

Shopping Practicalities

M adrid has something for all tastes and all budgets. You'll naturally find the big names, such as Zara and Promod, which are now found almost everywhere in Europe. You'll also find a multitude of local designers and manufacturers who experiment with fabrics and materials for their own pleasure and ours. Shoe-lovers will discover a fantastic choice of footwear. Others, young and old alike, will be able to splash out in the craft and antique shops.

WHERE TO SHOP

There are three main shopping districts in Madrid. If you're keen on luxury goods and ready-to-wear clothes, make for the Salamanca district. With its small shopping arcades and elegant, up-market boutiques selling classic designer clothes, shoes and accessories, it's a wonderful place to shop. If you like trendier styles and creative fashion by young designers, head for Calle Almirante and Calle Conde de Xiquena in the Chueca district. If you want to take home souvenirs of Spain, the area around Puerta del Sol is the place to go. There are food and wine markets throughout the city and don't miss the Rastro – one of the best fleamarkets in Europe, if not the world.

OPENING TIMES

The opening times of Spanish shops are enough to confuse anyone. Shops are generally open Monday to Friday, from 10am to 2pm and from 5 to

8pm and on Saturday mornings. In the Salamanca district, however, they stay open on Saturday afternoons, too. The small shopping arcades in the city centre and the department stores, on the other hand, are generally open Monday to Saturday from 10am to 9pm. Markets tend to be held in the mornings only.

FINDING YOUR WAY

Next to each address in the Shopping and Nightlife sections (pages 86-123) you'll find its location on the map of Madrid on pages 82-83.

SALES

There are two main sale periods, as there are in other parts of Europe. The first begins in the second week in January and ends at the start of February, while the second begins at the start of July and goes on until August. The prices can be very attractive, especially for makes such as Zara and Massimo Dutti. Outside these periods, however, many shops still have special offers.

HOW TO PAY

Virtually all shops take credit cards, especially Visa and Eurocard. For any other cards you may want to use, it's a good idea to check the stickers on shop windows. You simply present your card and sign the till receipt in the usual way. If you want to pay cash, you'll find cash machines (Télebanco, Servi Red, Argentaria and Caja España)

just about everywhere, These take Visa and Eurocard. A commission will be charged per transaction, so try to work out how much you'll need altogether and take it out in one go. Cheques are rarely accepted.

In the event of loss or theft of credit cards, call the relevant centre in Madrid.

American Express
☎ 91 572 03 03.

Visa/Eurocard/ Mastercard
☎ 91 519 21 00.

Diners
☎ 91 547 40 00.

PRICES

For the last few years, the prices in Spain have been rising until they are now much the same as elsewhere in Europe. There are therefore fewer good bargains to be had here than previously. However, some items, such as leather goods, are still very good value for money.

WEEKEND SHOPPING

All the shops are open on Saturday mornings (see opening times above). Sunday trading, on the other hand, is usually restricted to bakeries, pastry shops and newspaper kiosks, so you'll have to fall back on the Rastro (see page 48), the only shopping area open in the city. This is where you'll find the biggest open-air flea market in Spain. It's only held on Sundays and holidays from 9am to 2pm, but you can find all sorts of unusual objects here.

CUSTOMS

If you're an EU citizen, you won't have to pay customs duty on your purchases, but you will have to show the receipts when you cross the border. You'll also need to provide a description of your purchases, together with your name and address. Non-EU citizens are exempt from paying VAT on purchases with a value of over €90 or those made in shops affiliated to the CashBack service. It's essential to ask for a CashBack refund form at the time of purchase. On leaving Spain, make sure you have the forms stamped by customs, then send them to the Cashback service. No VAT exemption is available for Europe.

SHIPPING YOUR PURCHASES HOME

If you buy a bulky object, you can easily have it shipped home. Just give the transportation company a copy of your invoice so that they can make out the delivery note and they'll take care of the rest.

UPS
☎ 900 102 410.

SEUR
☎ 91 322 80 00.

If you buy a work of art or an antique declared as *de valor patrimonial* (of national value), you must request an export licence from the Spanish equivalent of the National Heritage. The vendor will be able to help you with this process.

WOMEN'S FASHION

The *Movida* – the dawn of an artistic and cultural freedom in the 1970s – gave birth to an important generation of Spanish designers, most of whom settled in Madrid. Names such as Adolfo Dominguez and Agatha Ruiz de la Prada succeeded in banishing stereotypes and introducing a stunning cocktail of colours and styles. Thanks to them, Madrid fashion is constantly changing and evolving. Their watchword is seeking out the new.

DESIGNERS

Adolfo Dominguez

Calle Serrano, 96 and 18 (C1)
☎ 91 576 70 53
or 91 577 82 80.

In 1979 the Galician designer Adolfo Dominguez launched a line of urban, prêt-à-porter clothes with the provocative slogan 'creases are beautiful'. These two shops sell his collection of smart, practical designs, fine accessories and jewellery. They offer excellent value for money for both men and women, which is good reason to pay a visit.

Purificacion Garcia

Calle Serrano, 92 and 28 (C1)
☎ 91 576 72 76 or
91 577 83 70
Mon.-Sat. 10am-8.30pm.

This designer from Galicia sells clothes for women, specialising in jackets that are suitable for everyday wear as well as for special occasions. The accent is on natural fibres and classic styling, and the clothes sell for affordable prices.

Agatha Ruiz de la Prada

Calle Marques de Riscal, 8 (C1)
☎ 91 310 44 83
Mon.-Fri. 10am-2pm, 5-8pm,
Sat. 10am-2pm.

If a classic look isn't your thing, here at last are some original, even slightly eccentric, collections. Agatha Ruiz de la Prada, an experienced designer, first made her mark in the winter of 1998 in Paris, with designs combining natural plants and flowers. The shop also sells perfumed candles, leather goods, writing paper and shower curtains in the same vein.

LEATHER AND SUEDE

Facciaro
Galeria ABC
Calle Serrano, 61 (C1)
☎ **91 578 01 99**
Mon.-Sat. 10am-9.30pm.

If you like leather and suede, don't pass this shop by. It sells shoes, bags, suede jackets and bomber jackets, and leather coats for both men and women, all at incredible prices (a suede jacket costs around €55). Don't worry if you can't make it to this particular outlet, there are many other shops belonging to the same chain in Madrid. Phone the above number for a list of addresses.

FUR

Elena Benarroch
Calle Jose Ortega y Gasset, 14 (D1)
☎ **91 435 51 44**
Mon.-Sat. 10am-2pm, 4.30-8.30pm.

If you like fur, you'll find 700m² (7,500 sq ft) of sheer luxury and refinement here. The ultra-sophisticated decor alone is worth coming for. Elena Benarroch has revolutionised the world of fur by updating the styles and cuts and bringing them into the 21st century. She sells her own collections in this shop, as well as other major brands of clothes and a large number of attractive accessories, including hats, scarves, perfume and Santa Maria Novella soap.

Antonio Pernas
Calle Claudio Coello, 46 (D1)
☎ **91 578 16 76**
Mon.-Sat. 10am-2pm, 5-8.30pm.

This shop's stark but refined interior was designed by the architect Lago Seara. Its lines echo the minimalist characteristics of the last collections of the Freire-Pernas partnership. The traditional, functional clothes combine a good cut and quality fabrics, and the menswear collection is a recent addition to the range.

Roberto Torreta
Calle Jorge Juan, 14 (C/D1)
☎ **91 435 79 89**
Mon.-Sat. 10.30am-2pm, 5-8.30pm.

If you're smart with a modern outlook, you're just the kind of woman this designer likes to dress. This shop, at the end of a little street, sells fairly classic clothes including a large range of jackets made of such diverse fabrics as linen and leather. There are some really lovely items, but the prices are generally quite high. Expect to pay around €235-400 for an outfit.

HIGH-STREET FASHION

Vilagallo

Calle Hermosilla, 35 (D1)
☎ 91 577 33 17
**Mon.-Sat. 10am-2pm,
5-8pm.**

Jackets, jackets and still more jackets! The cut is generally classic, and all the models come in a choice of top-quality fabrics and a number of different lengths, not to mention an incredible range of patterns and colours. All kinds of combinations are possible, with waistcoats and scarves to complete your outfit as an added bonus. The prices are reasonable, ranging from around €120-150.

Massimo Dutti

Calle Velázquez, 46 (off map)
☎ 91 431 77 90
Calle Goya, 73 (D1)
☎ 91 431 39 00
Mon.-Sat. 10am-8pm.

These two shops stay open between 2 and 5pm, which is very unusual in Madrid. The off-the-peg range favours the current trend for natural fabrics. The shops are part of the Zara group (see right), but the clothes they sell are of better quality. This is to a certain extent reflected in the price, though the clothes are still very affordable.

Zara

**Calle Princesa, 45 and 63 (A1)
Gran Vía, 32 (B2)
Calle Preciados, 20 and 14
Fuencarral, 126-128
Mon.-Sat. 10am-8.30pm.**

You may already have encountered this popular chain of shops selling clothes for all the family in other parts of Europe. Prices are very reasonable and there's a wide choice on offer, so there's really no need to hesitate.

Cortefiel

Gran Vía, 27-76 (B2)
☎ 91 522 00 93
Mon.-Sat. 10am-8.30pm.

These shops were established in the 1980s and specialise in inexpensive sportswear and streetwear. They sell a classic doubleknit lambswool jumper that comes in a wide range of colours and a young line that goes under the name of Springfield (Gran Vía 59).

ZARA, A FASHION PHENOMENON

Since it opened, Zara has brought about a fashion revolution. It has dozens of outlets throughout Spain, and the brand has been just as successful in other parts of Europe and the United States. Its success is based on the sale of up-to-the-minute collections at incredibly low prices. The Zara designers adapt their styles to customer demand as well as the latest trends and they are constantly bringing out new ranges throughout the season. Zara also sells clothes for the rest of the family at prices that are quite irresistible.

A NEW LEASE OF LIFE FOR THE *MANTON DE MANILLA*

This shawl, which originated in China, arrived in Spain in 1821 by way of Manila in the Philippines, which was at that time a Spanish colony. The popular silk or crêpe shawl with colourful, hand-embroidered designs and long fringes was considered a vital accessory for the streetwear or a bullfight. Two centuries later, it's been revamped and brought up to date by designers such as Moschino, Givenchy and Victoris & Lucchino. It's now considered the height of chic to drape one round your shoulders.

Glam

Calle Fuencarral, 35 (B1)
☎ 91 522 80 54
**Mon.-Sat. 10am-2pm,
5-9pm.**

If you're into trendy 70s clothes, you certainly won't be disappointed by this amazing psychedelic shop or, for that matter, any of the others in the neighbourhood. The street is overflowing with shops selling platform shoes, flared trousers, clinging knitted dresses, miniskirts, hotpants and gold and silver boob-tubes that are definitely only for the young and daring.

La Cebra

Calle Fuencarral, 43 (B1)
☎ 91 522 07 20
**Mon.-Sat. noon-2pm,
5-8.30pm.**

If you love partying, are proud of your body and have nothing to hide, then come along to La Cebra. With vinyl and sequins the order of the day, the clothes are provocative and extravagant. Add an extra touch of originality and recklessness and you get clinging dresses, sexy blouses and the shortest of

mini-skirts. If you want the perfect accessory for your revealing outfit, there's even a tattoo studio at your disposal!

LINGERIE

Oh! Que Luna

Calle Ayala, 32 (D1)
☎ 91 431 37 25
**Mon.-Sat. 10am-2pm,
5-8.30pm.**

The nightwear they sell here is both romantic and elegant. One of the oldest lingerie shops in Madrid, Oh! Que Luna sells pyjamas and nightdresses for little girls and women, as well as mules and wraps in a variety of pretty pastel shades. They're all made of soft, shimmering fabrics, such as panne velvet, moiré and wild silk. For a more simple, classic look they also stock beautiful cotton nightdresses that resemble those worn in Victorian times.

SHOES AND ACCESSORIES

The Spanish like to look their best and adore fashion accessories. From the most classic to the more eccentric, they add the finishing touch to any outfit. If you're in any doubt about making a purchase, the competitive prices and sheer variety on offer should help you to make up your mind.

Camper
Calle Preciados, 23 (B2)
☎ 91 531 78 97
Mon.-Sat. 10am-8pm.

Designed for a young market and with the environment in mind, the Camper brand of shoes and boots is quickly gaining in popularity. New models are launched every year, but the classic designs with crêpe soles are still the most successful. There are Camper shops throughout Madrid, but this one has the best selection.

Ditomo
Calle Jose Ortega y Gasset, 19 (D1)
☎ 91 577 19 76
Mon.-Sat. 10.30am-2.30pm, 5-8.30pm.

This shop sells nothing but bags. And not just leather bags, but bags made of velvet, linen, silk and gauze, decorated with feathers and gemstones. Real attention to detail and originality goes into the making. Expect to pay €45-110 for a creation that you just won't find anywhere else.

Excrupulus Net
Calle Almirante (C1)
☎ 91 521 72 44
Mon.-Sat. 11am-2pm, 5-8.30pm.

These shoes and accessories by the Catalan designer Muxart are highly original, not to say unique. You won't find the like of them elsewhere. Some of the shoes even have jackets to match. Originality, however, comes at a price, but there are other excellent shoe and accessory shops on the same street.

Sophie
Calle Hermosilla, 37 (D1)
☎ 91 431 13 29
Mon.-Sat. 10am-2pm, 5-8.30pm.

In this amusingly-decorated shop, in shades of blue and green, the articles on sale form part of the decor. The gloves, hats, necklaces, bags (around €12-25) and ebony hair pins (from €5) are cleverly displayed according to the season, and form part of the backdrop. The prices blend into the background, too!

Piamonte

Calle Piamonte, 16 (C1)
☎ **91 522 45 80**
Mon.-Sat. 10am-2pm,
5-8.30pm.

If you have a dream bag
in mind, Piamonte can
probably make it. The
opening of this shop
was a minor revolution.
It sells made-to-order
bags at affordable
prices. It also stocks
a very fine collection
of silver jewellery
(the rings
are especially
beautiful) as well
as top-quality scarves,
belts and ties.

Marinoni

Calle Jorge Juan, 12
(C/D1)
☎ **91 577 25 21**
Mon.-Sat. 10.30am-2pm,
5-8.30pm.

Marinoni is aimed at elegant,
sophisticated women. Among
other things, you'll find the
perfect accessory you need to
match a smart dress or suit,
whether it's a handbag, shopping
bag, choker or earrings. They also
stock a selection of matching
shoes for women who want to
look their best.

Cristina Castañer

Calle Claudio Coello, 51 (D1)
☎ **91 578 18 90**
Mon.-Sat. 10.30am-2pm,
5-8.30pm.

This shop sells the famous
Spanish espadrille in every
conceivable colour, shade and
style, whether traditional, or more
sophisticated and elegant. Its
reputation and success are based
on them. It would be a mistake
to think they are only suitable
for the summer as the
winter collection is really
interesting, too. There
are also scarves, bags
and jewellery to go
with the shoes.

Mirta Gómez

Calle Lagasca, 62
(off map)
☎ **91 575 28 48**
Mon.-Sat. 10am-2pm,
5-8pm.

You won't find bright
colours or extravagant
designs at this shoe
shop, just the essential
basics – shoes for
men and women
that are so
comfortable you'll
want to wear them
day in and day
out. The prices
are very reasonable
as well (from €18).

SPANISH SHOE SIZES

Until recently, shoe sizes in
Spain were different from
those elsewhere in Europe.
For example, a Spanish 39 used
to equate to the continental
size 38. However, a short while
ago, the Spanish adopted the
European norm, though some
manufacturers are yet to
follow suit. For further
information on sizes, consult
the conversion tables on p. 126.

Calzados Cordones

Calle Santiago, 6 (A2)
☎ **91 547 78 32**
Mon.-Fri. 10am-2pm,
5-8pm, Sat. 10am-2pm.

If you can never find
shoes to fit because your
feet are an unusual
size, either large or
small, you'll find
them here. There are
classic, modern and
fashionable designs
in sizes 31-34 (girl's
size 11–women's size
1) and sizes 41-44
(8-11) for women and
46-51 (13-16) for men, all
at attractive prices (around
€42-72).

MEN'S FASHION

Spanish men are very fashion-conscious and like to look their best. Accessories, labels, designer clothes and monogrammed shirts are all regarded as signs of elegance. While the overall look remains classic in style, the new generation of designers are beginning to change men's habits by offering more modern fabrics and cuts.

The Tie Gallery

Calle Lagasca, 67 (off map)
☎ **91 577 97 23**
Mon.-Sat. 10am-2pm, 5-8pm.

This little shop specialises in a range of Italian silk ties. The raw materials come from Italy, but the ties are all made in Spain. They come in bright colours as well as pastel shades in dozens of relatively traditional designs. Prices range from around €18-33.

Zocco

Calle Fuencarral, 42 (B1)
☎ **91 523 49 33**
Mon.-Sat. 10am-2pm, 5-9pm.

If you like trendy clothes, this shop with its metallic decor will be a winner. You'll find clinging Lycra T-shirts and shirts on the first floor, along with sleeveless T-shirts and the latest jackets. Accessories (mainly bags and belts) and underwear are on the second floor.

Throttleman

Calle Ayala, 28 (D1)
☎ **91 577 87 92**
Mon.-Sat. 10am-2.30pm, 5-8.30pm.

This shop could have been called 'The Shirt Palace'. From traditional shirts for the office (with several styles of collar) to casual shirts for a streetwear look, every possible kind of shirt can be found here. They also have a good selection of accessories including ties (from €30), braces, belts and some 300 styles of underpants including boy's underpants (all at one price, €15).

Hombre de Hoy

Calle Infantas, 10 (B/C1)
☎ **91 522 30 73**
Mon.-Sat. 11am-2pm, 5-9pm.

Feeling tired and stressed? Then come and relax in this men-only beauty centre, where everything possible will be done to help you unwind and feel like a new man. They stock a full range of cosmetics, and offer hair removal, sunbeds and massage treatments.

Flip

Calle Mayor, 19 (B2)
☎ 93 366 44 72
Mon.-Sat. 10am-2pm, 5-8.30pm.

With over 100m²/sq yds of shopping space on offer, you'll be spoilt for choice when it comes to jeans, baseball caps and the very latest outfits for the young and trendy of Madrid. The shop sells mainly streetwear and sportswear, including makes such as Kangol.

Asuntos Internos

Calle Fuencarral, 2 (B1)
☎ 91 532 32 99
Mon.-Sat. 10am-2pm, 5-8.30pm.

This shop is entirely devoted to men's underwear. From the most classically elegant to the most modern and garish, you'll find plenty of gift ideas that are sure to please.

Zapatería Tenorio

Plaza de la Provincia, 6 (B2)
☎ 91 366 44 40
Mon.-Fri. 9.30am-1.30pm, 4.30-8pm, Sat. 9.30am-1.30pm.

Tradition is the watchword of the day at this little cobbler's, which smells enticingly of leather and polish. Made-to-measure riding boots have been hand-crafted here for generations. At around €600 a pair, they certainly don't come cheap, but their high price is justified by their impeccable quality.

ARTESANOS CAMISEROS

**Galeria ABC
Calle Serrano, 61,
tienda 119 (C1)**
☎ 91 575 97 27
Mon.-Sat. 10am-9.30pm.

If you want to have a shirt made to measure, then this is the place to come. There are over 300 fabrics to choose from, including poplin, cotton and linen, and a dozen different styles of collars, cuffs and pockets, with monogramming an optional extra. The prices vary with the fabrics (from €33-51). The shirts take a fortnight to make, however, for a €6 supplement, you can have yours ready in four days. The Artesanos Camiseros chain also sells underpants, pyjamas and cuff links.

A CHILD'S WORLD

With the birth rate one of the lowest in Europe, Spanish people tend to treat their children like royalty. When it comes to toys, clothes and parties, nothing is too good for them. They must always be *a la última* – kitted out in the latest fashion, with little girls dressed like princesses. Designer clothes for children can be very expensive and few shops sell tasteful clothes at affordable prices.

household accessories that go with them– tiny wooden utensils, miniature cast-iron saucepans, doll's prams and doll's houses. Little girls – and some older ones – will love them.

Afizonia

Calle Serrano, 100 (C1)
☎ **91 426 23 00**
Mon.-Fri. 10am-8.30pm,
Sat. 10am-3pm, 5-9pm.

Toys, books and construction kits for young and old alike. The paper construction kits of the great monuments of Madrid, such as Plaza de Toros (for the over-tens), are particularly interesting and make appropriate gifts to take home.

El Zapatito Inglés

Calle Don Ramón de la Cruz, 14 (D1)
☎ **91 577 96 97**
Mon.-Sat. 10.30am-2pm, 5-8pm.

As you walk down the narrow alleyway, on your right you'll see a small shop specialising in children's shoes. Usually made from leather, the majority of the shoes are of high quality. You can find good old English Start-Rites here, as well as the Italian make, Supergas. The rest of the shoes, including: Abetitos and Gulliver Pontiare, are Spanish.

Party City

Galeria ABC
Calle Serrano, 61 (C1)
☎ **91 576 17 55**
Mon.-Sat. 10am-9.30pm.

This is birthday party paradise. You'll find everything you could want here for the perfect children's party, from invitation cards and table decorations to all kinds of dressing-up clothes and party favours. If you've a birthday coming up in the family, this is definitely the ideal place for all your needs.

Imaginarium

Galeria ABC
Calle Serrano, 61 (C1)
Mon.-Sat. 10am-9.30pm.

All kinds of creative and intelligent toys for your children (from 3 months to 10 years), to help them develop and make learning fun. It's a good way to please everyone.

Así

Gran Vía, 47 (B2)
☎ **91 548 28 28**
Mon.-Sat. 10am-2pm, 4.30-8.30pm.

You can't walk round this shop without being dazzled by all the high-quality toys on offer, including beautiful china and collectors' dolls that you won't find anywhere else. Their wardrobes are amazing, not to mention all the

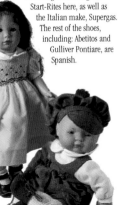

Miña

Calle Don Ramón de la Cruz, 14 (D1)
☎ 91 577 43 87
Mon.-Sat. 10.30am-2pm, 5-8.30pm.

Close by El Zapatito Ingles, you'll find a small shop selling very traditional clothes for babies and young children. These include smocked dresses in Liberty prints and pastel shades, tartan shorts and kilts. The *Scotch House* made in Spain!

Mothercare

Calle Claudio Coello, 44 (D1)
☎ 91 577 23 19
Mon.-Sat. 10am-8.30pm.

A branch of the world-famous children's retailers, they sell easy-going clothes for babies and children up to eight years.

The casual style is fairly rare in Madrid, where children's clothes are usually more sophisticated and classic. The shop sells a line of maternity wear and there's even a department for premature babies. From cradle to car seat, there's everything you need for a baby.

Boch

Calle Claudio Coello, 50 (D1)
☎ 91 575 28 98
Mon.-Sat. 10am-2pm, 5-8.30pm.

This chain of shops has six outlets dotted about the city. You'll find the big names of children's fashion here, including Naf-Naf, Cacharel, Chevignon, Kenzo and Ralph Lauren. Good taste at high prices.

WHERE TO GO WITH YOUR CHILDREN

If you want to make your children's stay in Madrid an unforgettable one, you'll find some great ideas below.

Museo de Ferrocarril

Paseo de las Delicias, 61 (C3)
☎ 902 22 88 22
Tue.-Sun. 10am-3pm
Entry charge.

A collection of 33 trains, housed in a marvellous building. Steam engines, diesel locomotives and period carriages all await you, along with miniature trains.

El Zoo Aquarium

Casa de Campo (off map)
☎ 91 711 99 50

Every day 10am-8.30pm
Metro Batán or taxi
Entry charge.

Children will adore this zoo, where they can discover the rare and endangered white tiger and see exhibitions of dolphins and birds of prey (ask the times on the way in). As for the aquarium, it's quite out of this world.

Parque de Atracciones

Casa de Campo (off map)
☎ 91 463 64 33 or
91 463 29 00
Entry charge.

The park offers attractions galore, as well as shows and all manner of delights to please your children and make their stay in the city both exciting and fun.

SPORT

Apart from football, which has always got everyone's vote, the Spanish have never been renowned for their great interest in sport. Over the past few years, however, a new trend has been emerging. There's a new willingness to participate in sports of all kinds in order to stay fit and healthy. The nearby ski resorts and nature reserves are an added incentive to physical exercise.

Avant Sport

Calle Carnero, 10 (A/B3)
☎ 91 468 72 22
Mon.-Sat. 10am-2pm, 5-8pm,
Sun. 10am-2pm.

Avant Sport is one of a number of similar small shops in this street which specialise in hiking and skiing equipment. If you're planning to go on an excursion, you can find all the essentials here, including goose-down anoraks, waterproof suits, walking boots, rucksacks and sleeping bags of the very best quality.

Deportes Koala

Calle León, 29 (B2)
☎ 91 429 91 89
Mon.-Fri. 10am-1.45pm,
5-8.15pm, Sat. 10am-1.45pm.

Hiking, mountaineering and potholing enthusiasts will find an amazing range of top-quality equipment here, including ice-axes, ropes, goggles, boots and all the accessories necessary for survival in extreme conditions.

Army & Navy Stores

Calle Carnero, 5 (A/B3)
☎ 91 530 28 48
Mon.-Fri. 10am-2pm, 5-8pm,
Sat.-Sun. 9.30am-2pm.

With the range of compasses, binoculars, torch lights, survival blankets, jackets and other useful and essential objects on sale here, this shop is a call to travel and adventure. And just in case you're interested, it even sells camouflage cream for those occasional night-time manoeuvres!

San Francisco Skate Farm

Calle Argensola, 3 (C1)
☎ 91 319 14 55
Mon.-Sat. 10am-2pm, 5-8.30pm.

If you're more inclined to skateboard than walk up and down the streets of Madrid, you'll find this shop of interest. Behind the old wooden façade, it has a wide choice of skateboards, along with all the essential accessories.

Dak-Tak

**Calle Hilarión Eslava, 44
(off map)
☎ 91 544 76 04
Mon.-Fri.
10am-2pm,
5-8pm, Sat.
10am-2pm.**

Fans
of surf-
boarding
and snow-
boarding
will love this
specialised shop.
Summer and winter
alike, it has the best
range of boarding
equipment in the
whole of Spain.
It also has a workshop,
which can prove very
useful.

El Caballo

**Calle Lagasca, 55 (off map)
☎ 91 576 40 37
Mon.-Sat. 10am-2pm,
5-8pm.**

This shop is a horse-rider's
paradise. Everything remotely
connected with equestrianism
can be found here, from saddles
and crops to specialised riding
clothes, including boots, jackets
and jodhpurs. The first floor
houses a fine collection of
traditional leather goods (bags
and shoes) of the very highest
quality.

Fútbol Total

**Calle Eloy Gonzalo, 7
(off map)
☎ 902 442 433
Mon.-Sat. 10am-2pm,
5-8pm.**

This shop is ideal for football
fanatics as it sells the official
strips of all the world's leading
football clubs, not to mention
the accessories needed to take part
in the sport. Expect to pay €55
for a Real Madrid child's strip
(including shirt, shorts and socks)
or a Barça adult's shirt.

CORONEL TAPIOCA

**Calle Serrano, 81 (C1)
☎ 91 563 22 21
Calle Hermosilla, 31 (D1)
☎ 91 576 22 88
Mon.-Sat. 10am-2pm,
5-8pm.**

If you're planning a desert
safari, or you see yourself
as a fearless explorer from
Raiders of the Lost Ark, then
you'll find everything you
could possibly need for your
adventure at Coronel Tapioca.
They sell waistcoats with
plenty of pockets, penknives,
torches, water bottles and
travel bags, as well as
sportswear for the city, all at
affordable prices.

Paz Sport Station

**Calle Fuencarral,
41 (B1)
☎ 91 523 21 80
Mon.-Sat. 11am-
2pm, 5-9pm.**

This is *the* specialist shop for
trainers and sports shoes. Whether
you want to take part in your
favourite sport or simply complete
your casual look, you'll find
examples of all the fashionable
makes here – Nike, Converse,
Adidas, New Balance and the rest.
It could also be a useful port of
call if you're planning a long
day's walking in Madrid.

CRAFTS

Whether ceramics, leather or jewellery, today's Spanish craft has lost none of its appeal. On the contrary, an incredible variety of contemporary pieces can be found alongside antique designs and reproductions and many Spanish master craftsmen have earned worldwide recognition.

beautiful ceramics including classic tureens, jugs, dishes and tea sets. This antiquated shop sells a wide selection of their work, as well as a large number of reproductions of antique designs. Expect to pay around €5 for a glass or a handpainted bowl.

Adamá
Avda Felipe II, 24 (off map)
☎ **91 435 99 88**
**Mon.-Sat. 10am-2pm,
4.30-8.30pm.**

Cantaro
Calle Flor Baja, 8 (A1)
☎ **91 547 95 14**
**Mon.-Sat. 10am-2pm,
5-9pm.**

The articles in this popular ceramics shop are arranged on two floors and classified according to their region of origin (Seville, Grenada, Valencia, etc.). Not only are they fine examples of their art, but, surprise, surprise, they're affordable, too.

Antigua Casa Talavera
**Calle Isabel La Católica, 2
(A1)**
☎ **91 547 34 17**
**Mon.-Fri. 10am-1.30pm,
5-8pm, Sat. 10am-1.30pm.**

The workshops of Talavera, a small town in the neighbourhood of Toledo, are renowned for their

Chauia
**Calle Ribera de Curtidores,
33 (B3)**
☎ **91 527 52 25**
**Mon.-Fri. 10.30am-2pm,
5-8pm, Sat.-Sun. 10.30am-
2pm.**

An excellent place to stock up on presents at reasonable prices, you'll find all sorts of ceramic objects here in traditional shades of blue and white, including sugar bowls, water jugs, salad bowls and even umbrella stands.

If you like ceramics but are tired of the traditional designs and patterns and are looking for something more original, then this is the place for you. The work of the 40 most important contemporary craftsmen (Alberto Hernandez, Rafa Perez and others) can be found here. You'll find lots of bright colours, unusual lampstands and all kinds of tableware.

Concha Garcia

Calle Goya, 38 (D1)
☎ 91 435 49 36
Mon.-Sat. 10.30am-2.30pm, 4.30-8.30pm.

This shop sells antique, ethnic and original jewellery, as well as a range of designs by such artists as Joaquim Berao and Joan Miró. The ebony necklaces and fabulous chokers are definitely worth a look. With earrings priced from around €12, you'll find an amazing range of jewellery on offer at perfectly affordable prices.

Capa Esculturas

Calle Claudio Coello, 19 (D1)
☎ 91 431 03 65
Mon.-Sat. 10am-2pm, 5-8pm.

This gallery displays the work of 26 highly talented young Spanish sculptors, all at the cutting edge of modern art. The pieces, often in bronze, represent abstract and figurative forms, varying from the provocative to more quiet, introspective works. Production costs are kept to a minimum and prices range from €84 to around €2,400. If you're an art lover or

a collector, this is the place to come to see the latest trends.

Lola Fonseca

Calle Santa Isabel, 50 (C3)

☎ 91 530 65 22
Mon.-Fri. 10am-2pm, 4.30-8.30pm, Sat. 10am-2pm.

This appealing and original shop and workshop offers a large selection of handpainted silk shawls, ties, bow ties and scarves (from around €33). The shawls are particularly tempting, with attractive geometrical and oriental patterns, reproductions of famous monuments, and unusual designs on themes including 'day and night', 'grass and sand', and 'spider and fly'. You can also have the design of

your choice reproduced on a piece of silk to use in any way you please.

Calle Conde de Xiquena, 13 (C1)
☎ 91 310 16 20

You'd think you were in an art gallery from the way the jewellery in this shop is displayed. Joaquín Berao has made a name for himself working in silver and takes his inspiration from nature, although he's now turned his hand to some gold pieces. Don't leave without seeing his beautiful solid silver bracelets (from €288) and small patinated bronze vases (for around €168).

Tikal

Calle Hileras, 9 (B2)
☎ 91 558 11 85
Mon.-Sat. 10am-2pm, 5-8pm.

When you step inside this shop, you're immediately struck by the strong perfumed smell of incense. You'll find all kinds of craft objects from Central and South America here, including picture frames., mirrors, boxes and lamps but by far the most interesting are the little-known board games from Asia and the Middle East. They certainly make a change from computer games.

ANTIQUES AND SECONDHAND

The *Madridleños* don't seem to go in much for conserving objects from their past. It's difficult to find many true Spanish antiques and there are few good finds to be made in the rustic Iberian style in secondhand shops. Antique dealers often have to look abroad to satisfy their clients.

Bravo
Callejon del Mellizo, 7 (A3)
☎ **91 366 32 47**
Every day 9.30am-1.30pm.

This is a real old-fashioned junk shop, with piles of interesting objects and bits and pieces lying about everywhere. If you delve about a bit, you should be able to come up with old postcards, clocks and even the odd *mantone de Manilla*, the brightly-embroidered shawl worn by Spanish women.

Kumquat
Calle Hermosilla, 44 (D1)
☎ **91 577 52 30**
Mon.-Fri. 10.30am-2pm, 5-8pm, Sat. 11am-2pm.

Angel
Calle Carlos Arniches, 4 (B3)
☎ **91 528 63 05**
Every day 10.30am-1.30pm.

Angel is another specialist shop, but this time for frames. Large or small, round or square, oval or rectangular, there really is something to suit all tastes here, with a definite emphasis on gilding. If your suitcase is too small for one of the larger frames, fall back on a little photo frame just right for a family portrait.

Ropa Epoca
Calle Carnero, 10 (B3)
Tue.-Sun. noon-2pm, 6-8pm.

Ropa Epoca is a shop specialising in old clothes and costumes. It offers a very wide choice, provided you're looking for something dating pre-1960s. Some of the clothes are made out of beautiful, delicate fabrics, such as organdie and silk, while others are traditional costumes from Andalusia and Madrid.

A fairly traditional shop with a predominance of British furniture, as well as a wide choice of porcelain dinner services, small frames, statuettes, paintings, and bronze and marble lamps (from around €150). If you don't want to break open the piggy bank, you can also find good reproductions of antiques here at more affordable prices.

Centro de Anticuarios Lagasca

Calle Lagasca, 36 (off map)
Mon.-Sat. 11am-2pm,
5-8.30pm, Sat. 11am-2pm.

A number of well-known antique dealers are grouped together in this gallery. There are many very fine things for sale, but unfortunately they're also more or less the most expensive that Madrid has to offer. It's worth coming, though, just for the pleasure of browsing.

V Dinastía

Calle Lope de Vega, 22 (C2)
☎ 91 420 11 67
Mon.-Fri. 10am-2pm, 4.30-8pm, Sat. 11am-2pm.

All the furniture and *objets d'art* on sale here come from China and Korea. There are many fine pieces of lacquerwork and items that you rarely see elsewhere, such as a superb palanquin (litter) lacquered in shades of red, yellow and green (around €1,560), Korean wooden chests and boxes, and a variety of screens. Perfect if you like exotic furniture.

Almoneda

Calle Lagasca, 38 (off map)
☎ 91 576 21 06
Mon.-Fri. 11am-2pm,
5-8.30pm, Sat. 11am-2pm.

Here the accent is definitely on quality rather than quantity. Even if you can't afford to buy the beautiful pieces of furniture, chandeliers and antique dolls on display, you can still come along just to admire them. To give you some idea of price, a wardrobe from this shop costs in the region of €2,100.

Mexico

Calle Huertas, 17 and 20 (B/C2)
☎ 91 429 94 76
Mon.-Fri. 10am-2pm, 5-8pm, Sat. 10am-2pm.

The whole world is represented in these two shops, located opposite one another on the Calle Huertas. The 16th to early 20th-century engravings are classified according to theme, with panoramic views, maps and costumes etc., all very reasonably priced at between €30 and €90.

Reciclass

Calle San Gregorio, 3 (C1)
☎ 91 310 27 92
Mon.-Fri. 10.30am-2pm, 5-8.30pm, Sat. 10.30am-2pm.

The owners of this shop have come up with a concept that's unique in Madrid. The items on display are the result of numerous visits to secondhand shops and flea markets for furniture of the 60s, 70s and 80s. Recycled and renovated with colourful fabrics and modern materials, their finds are converted into contemporary, stylish furniture. It's all very clever stuff.

INTERIOR DECORATION

The Spanish don't entertain at home much, so it's difficult to find out what their houses are like. However, if the growth of interior decoration shops of recent years, and the abundance of designer objects on sale in the stores is anything to go by, interior decoration is booming. As you'll see, the people of Madrid have a marked preference for bright colours and warm, natural materials, such as wood and linen. Combining traditional craft objects and contemporary furniture is also very popular.

Musgo

Galeria ABC
Calle Serrano, 61 (C1)
☎ **91 577 88 62**
Mon.-Sat. 10am-9.30pm.

There are Galeria ABC shops all over Madrid. Inside, you'll find a wealth of gift ideas, including decorative items, furniture (mainly cane or wrought iron) and futuristic kitchenware that's both attractive and useful – in other words, plenty to choose from for yourself or to take home as presents. It's also worth taking a look at their collection of clothes for women and children, leather goods and costume jewellery.

Natura Selection

Galeria ABC
Calle Serrano, 61 (C1)
☎ **91 575 96 81**
Mon.-Sat. 10am-9.30pm.

A visit to Natura Selection will add an exotic note to your trip. First, you'll be greeted by the perfume of incense, then you'll get the opportunity to buy all sorts of ethnic knick-knacks, including frames, baskets, lamps and scarves, all at prices that would please any hippy. The large, round creamy-coloured candles could well catch your eye (from around €8).

El Mercado Portugues

Calle General Oráa, 27
☎ **91 563 52 80**
Mon.-Sat. 10am-2pm, 5-8pm.

As the name of the shop suggests, items from Portugal have pride of place here. Everything on sale at El Mercado Portugues comes from Spain's close neighbour. From the ceramic tableware to the attractive tablecloths and household linen, there's a wealth of traditional Portuguese crafts that will add a touch of Lisbon to your home.

Barri Twice

**Calle General Arrando, 36
(off map)
☎ 91 308 67 43
Mon.-Fri. 10am-2pm,
4.30-8.30pm, Sat. 10.30am-
2pm, 5-8pm.**

Vinçon

**Calle Castelló, 18 (off map)
☎ 91 578 05 20
Mon. 5-8pm, Tue.-Sat.
10am-2pm, 5-8.30pm.**

This shop, located at the end of
a narrow alleyway, is housed in
a former factory that's been given
a loft-style makeover. A showcase
for young designers, Vinçon not
only gives them practical help
but also places a good deal of
the shop at their disposal. The
futuristic-looking objects all
have their use – it's up to you to
work out what it is! Have a look
at the lamps, which come in a
range of prices to suit all budgets
(from €30 to €420). There's
also a marvellous display of
children's toys that you won't
find anywhere else.

Bakuba

**Galeria ABC
Calle Serrano, 61 (C1)
☎ 91 575 63 26
Mon.-Sat. 10am-9.30pm.**

If you have an interest in African
and primitive art, this is a shop
you really shouldn't miss.
You'll find it hard to choose
between the magnificent
masks (from
around €70),
the colourful,
woven
textiles
and the
unusual
statuettes.

Artesanos
del Nuevo
Mundo

**Calle Castelló, 24
(off map)
☎ 91 435 67 79
Mon.-Sat. 11am-2.30pm,
5-8.30pm.**

This shop has a large display
area, which makes it easier
to make your choice from the
selection of beautiful ceramics
that you encounter as you walk
round. Surrounded by rustic
furniture and other items
from Mexico, you'll really
feel as though you have
been transported to a
new world.

You
really
must
make
sure you
drop in on
this New York-
style bazaar,
hidden away in a
basement. Everything
from the evening
clothes to the
decorative objects
is chosen with
great taste and
with quality
uppermost in
mind. They
even have unusual
Mexican ceramic
handbasins on
sale at very
competitive prices
(around €96
for a small
handbasin
and €132 for
a large one.

La Casa Julia

Calle Almirante, 1 (C1)
☎ **91 522 02 70**
**Mon.-Sat. 10am-2pm,
5-8.30pm.**

This shop run by designers is
devoted to original ethnic objects.
The owners have also just
launched their own collection
of teak and antique wooden
furniture. It's definitely worth
paying a visit.

Maison Folle

Calle San Marcos, 37 (C2)
☎ **91 521 98 97**
**Mon.-Fri. 10.30am-2pm,
5-8.30pm, Sat. 10.30am-
2pm.**

This establishment could have
ended up looking just like a
warehouse, yet the 400m² (4,500
sq ft) of exhibition space has been
arranged to very good effect.
Colonial-style furniture is much
in evidence, but interesting
glass, wood and wrought-iron
ornaments and decorative objects
are also on sale.

El Patio de Marta

**Calle Zurbano, 25
off map)**
☎ **91 308 08 02**
**Mon.-Fri. 10am-2pm,
5-8.30pm, Sat.
10.30am-2pm.**

You're bound to fall for
El Patio de Marta's wide
range of furniture and accessories,
made from a range of materials
including cane, teak and wrought
iron. The ceramic plates and the
little Moroccan-inspired mosaic
tiled tables (from around €450)
are particularly attractive.

ARTESPAÑA

Calle Hermosilla, 14 (D1)
☎ **91 435 02 21**
**Mon.-Sat. 10.15am-2pm,
5-8.30pm.**

Artespaña is a nationwide
company offering a whole
range of products made by
Spanish craftsmen. The large
selection of furniture in this
huge shop includes chests of
drawers, sideboards, shelves
and tables, as well as lamps,
vases and many different
kinds of decorative accessories,
as well as household linen.
If you aren't yet familiar with
traditional
Spanish
crafts, this
is the ideal
place to
discover
them.

Dar

Travesia de Belen, 3 (A2)
☎ **91 310 52 46**
**Mon.-Fri. 10.30am-2pm,
5-8.30pm, Sat. 10.30am-
2pm.**

Dar is the Arab word for 'house', and all the objects on sale in this shop originate from Morocco. The fine Safi and Jaen ceramics, the unusual striped plates, the candlesticks encrusted with coloured stones (around €18) and the beautiful mosaic tiled tables (for around €162) will add a touch of the exotic to your home.

Ojo de Pez

**Calle Fuencarral,
43 (B1)**
☎ **91 522
11 44**
**Mon.-Fri.
11am-
2pm,
5-9pm, Sat.
11.30am-2pm,
5.30-8.30pm.**

An interesting mix of papier mâché statues, lava lamps, bags, costume jewellery and oddly-shaped frames can be found in this shop. It's the ideal place to find a unique, even kitsch present that you won't find anywhere else. Don't expect to come back to find matching items on sale here, as the stock is continually changing. It's this constant renewal that makes Ojo de Pez such fun.

Batavia

Calle Serrano Anguita, 4 (B1)
☎ **91 448 75 63**
**Mon.-Sat. 10am-2.30pm,
5-8.30pm.**

Whether antique or modern, chests, tables or chairs, all the furniture here is made of teak and some is quite valuable. For a touch of the Orient in your home, you could choose some lacquered wooden baskets from China, or a beautiful shawl – especially as they can arrange to deliver the goods to your home address.

La Compania Z Importadora

Calle Serrano, 78 (C1)
☎ **91 435 32 26**
**Mon.-Sat. 10am-2pm,
4.30-8pm.**

With an attractive decor of ochre walls and a fountain, this shop makes you yearn to travel to exotic places. The fabrics, furniture and decorative objects on sale here all hail from India and Asia. The wooden furniture and the tableware are particularly beautiful. If you don't want to load yourself down too much, there is also a host of small knick-knacks that will fit into a suitcase!

EL KILO AMERICANO

**Calle Velázquez, 72
(off map)**
☎ **91 576 01 63**
Mon.-Sat. 11am-8pm.

El Kilo Americano sells top-quality, tastefully-designed fabrics, in every conceivable shade and colour, all at very reasonable prices. Madrid has nine such shops in all and every month, one of the fabric ranges is replaced in order to keep the stock up-to-date and to ensure variety. The upholstery service is worth considering, as it's very competitively priced.

SOUVENIRS AND CURIOSITIES

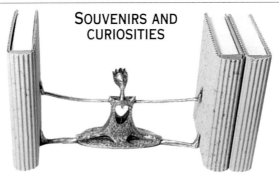

You can easily bring a pair of castanets, a tambourine or a Spanish costume doll back with you from Madrid, but when you spend a few days in the city, you'll soon realise there are plenty of other more original souvenirs available. They may be less traditional, but they're certainly more interesting. Here are some suggestions that may entice you.

Souvenirs

Calle Postas, 20 (B2)
☎ 91 366 48 59
Mon.-Sat. 11am-2pm, 5-10pm.

At last, a souvenir shop where you can actually buy something you would want to take home. There are one or two horrors, but plenty of good ideas as well, including wooden postcards, figurines (in various sizes) of the famous Spanish bull, Osborne, some really lovely T-shirts, old postcards, saffron, and mugs with reproductions of paintings by Picasso, Miró and others. You're sure to find something you like.

Palacios y Museos

Calle Velázquez, 47 (off map)
☎ 91 577 42 01
Mon.-Sat. 10am-9pm.

A little like a museum shop, over 1,500 art and culture-related objects are on sale on the two floors of this large shop. Among all the jewellery, leather goods, scarves, games and writing paper on offer, the umbrellas with reproductions of paintings really stand out.

Casa de Diego

Puerta del Sol, 12 (B2)
☎ 91 522 66 43
Mon.-Sat. 9.45am-1.30pm, 4.30-8pm.

This typically Spanish establishment, founded in 1858, is now the leading shop of its kind. It sells a wide variety of traditional fans, some of them incredibly beautiful (prices range from €210 to €300 for examples that are handpainted or inlaid with mother-of-pearl). There are also *mantones de Manila* – the beautiful Spanish fringed shawls – and parasols, which are worth a look for the quality of the work alone.

Curiosity Shop

Calle Latoneros, 1 (B2)
☎ 91 365 84 22
Mon.-Sat. 10.30am-2pm, 5-9pm.

The spirit of Dickens' *The Old Curiosity Shop* lives on in this place, which overflows with unique and original gifts. With the emphasis on nostalgia, magic and fantasy, you'll find crystal balls, special-effect lamps, clocks, mobiles, unusual umbrellas, distorting spectacles, gadgets and plenty more besides.

Los Caprichos de Goya

Calle Goya, 50 (entrance in Calle General Pardiñas-D1)
☎ 91 575 54 82
Mon.-Sat. 10am-2pm, 5-8pm.

The ultimate party shopping experience – 100m² (1,000 sq ft) of original presents, party favours and dressing-up outfits to surprise and amuse your guests. If you're planning a particular celebration, with over 5,000 items on offer in

Casa Jiménez

Calle Preciados, 42 (B2)
☎ 91 548 05 26
Mon.-Sat. 10.30am-1.30pm, 5.30-8pm.

This very old emporium specialises in *mantones de Manilla*, silk mantillas and other exquisite accessories of the kind. Their finest *mantones*, which are often very colourful, are hand made and can sell for up to €270. There are others of course, that are a little less expensive, if you're keeping an eye on your budget.

MATY

Calle Maestre Victoria, 2 (B2)
☎ 91 531 32 91 or 91 531 03 22
Mon.-Fri. 10am-2pm, 5-8pm, Sat. 10am-2pm.

Fans of flamenco will think they've entered Aladdin's Cave. This is a chance to buy a real Andalusian dress, either off the peg or made to measure. The ground floor of the shop is devoted to dance costumes, while the first floor offers a range of accessories and hundreds of dressing-up outfits.

one place, you'll find everything you could possibly need here to make your party really go with a swing.

Casa Postal

Calle Libertad, 37 (C2)
☎ 91 532 70 37
Mon.-Fri. 9.30am-2pm, 4.30-8.30pm, Sat. 9.30am-2pm.

Casa Postal is the ideal place for anyone who is interested in collecting old postcards. There are over 500,000 views from all over Spain here, and 25,000 of the capital alone. They all date from pre-1940 and you can even consult the catalogue published by the owner of the shop. They certainly make a change from the usual postcards you send home!

Maravillas

Calle de la Sal, 3 (B2)
☎ 91 366 52 48
Mon.-Sat. 10am-2pm, 5-8pm.

Pay a visit to this wonderful costumiers and prepare to be transported to another world. Surrounded by all the fabulous dresses from Seville, traditional regional costumes and Andalusian outfits, you just might decide to dress up as Carmen for the evening.

DEPARTMENT STORES AND SHOPPING ARCADES

The leading department store in Madrid is without a doubt El Corte Inglés. This huge chain has branches throughout the city and offers more and more goods and services on a daily basis. However, the latest trend is towards smaller-scale shopping arcades, which are springing up all over the city centre.

El Jardín de Serrano
Calle Goya, 6-8 (D1)
☎ **91 577 00 12**
Mon.-Sat. 10am-9.30pm.

This shopping centre, located in the heart of the Salamanca district, won the European design prize in its category. Though modest in size, it has a well-balanced concentration of elegant and up-market shops, such as Cerruti, Baby Duck (for children), Carla (perfume and cosmetics), Romero (stationery), Acanto (leather menswear) and Lottusse (shoes and accessories).

Vips
Gran Vía, 43 (B2)
Fuencarral, 101
Every day 9-3am.

This small, useful shopping centre is open practically 24 hours a day. There are a dozen other branches dotted about the city. If you're feeling a little hungry, come along to the restaurant or grocery department to buy a snack. If you want to have some photos developed, find a book, newspaper, plan of Madrid or toy, Vips is here to help you out and perform any number of essential services.

Sepu
Gran Vía, 32 (B2)
☎ **91 522 11 38**
Mon.-Sat. 10am-9.30pm.

If you're the kind of person who enjoys rummaging around for a bargain, *Sepu* is definitely the department store for you. Just down the street from Vips, here you'll find two floors of clothes, decorative objects and accessories for every room in the house, perfumes, cosmetics, toys and books. The prices are all very reasonable, but you can't always count on the quality.

Multicentro Serrano 88
Calle Serrano, 88 (C1)
Mon.-Sat. 10am-9pm.

This is one of the very first mini-shopping centres to have opened in the city. All kinds of shops are represented here, from fashion and giftware to the work of the famous Catalan jeweller, Tous, who sells both real and costume jewellery. There's even a cafeteria, in case you're feeling hungry.

Moda Shopping

**Avenida General
Perón, 40 (off map)
☎ 91 581 15 25
Every day
10am-8.30pm.**

This vast
shopping centre,
with its beautiful glass
roof, has over 70 stores,
including fashion, toy,
jewellery, and perfume
and cosmetics outlets.
On Sundays, only the
cafeterias, bars,
newspaper kiosks,
bookshops and temporary
exhibition rooms are open.

Mallorca

**Calle Velázquez (off map)
☎ 91 431 99 09
Every day
10am-9pm.**

Mallorca is a chain
of high-quality delicatessens,
with branches to be found all over
the city. They sell a range of
delicious cooked dishes, pastries,
cheese, ham and even a good
selection of wines. If you need to
make a last-minute purchase, on
any day of the week including
Sunday, this is the best place to
come. The prices may be a little
high, but at least you can be sure
of the quality.

Asca

**Paseo de la
Castellana,
79 (off map)
Mon.-Sat.
10am-
9pm.**

If you
are in a
hurry, or don't
much care for
window-shopping,
you'll find all
the big names in
Spanish and
foreign fashion
concentrated in
this 200 hectare/500 acre-
site in the middle of the
business district –
which means there's
plenty to choose from
if you're thinking of buying
a new wardrobe.

THE BOOM IN SHOPPING CENTRES

Over the last few years,
there has been an
explosion of small shopping
complexes in the centre of
Madrid and giant ones outside
the city. The latest shopping
centre to open is the very
trendy shopping centre in
Calle Fuencarral. Nevertheless,
the people of Madrid are
creatures of habit and don't
completely desert their local
businesses and the quantity of
covered markets throughout
the city are proof of this.

El Corte Inglés

**Calle Preciados, 1-2-3-4
(B2)
Calle Goya, 76-87 (D1)
☎ 91 379 80 00
Mon.-Sat. 10am-9.30pm.**

Corte Inglés, which was only
a simple little shop at the
beginning of the 20th century,
has turned into a veritable empire
with dozens of outlets (there
are 16 in Madrid alone). The
disappearance of its competitor,
Las Galerías Preciados, a few years
ago gave it a monopoly. Each store
has everything you could possibly
want or need, including a beauty
parlour, a cafeteria, a restaurant,
a travel agency, departments for
clothes, music, toys, books, videos,
and even a supermarket.

BOOKSHOPS

There are not many small, local bookshops in Madrid, and the ones that do exist often tend to be specialised. You'll find the best selection of books at El Corte Inglés or Cristol, even though they aren't exclusively bookshops. However, the recent opening of a branch of FNAC in the city centre has breathed new life into the book market.

De Viaje

Calle Serrano, 39 (C1)
☎ 91 577 98 99
Mon.-Fri. 10.30am-2pm, 5-8pm.

This hypermarket and travel agency has a considerable number of books connected with travel on offer. You can find every conceivable travel guide here. The selection on Madrid and the surrounding area is extremely good, and will certainly inspire you to make another visit. You can also take the opportunity to stock up on bags and travel accessories here.

Metrópolis

Calle Luna, 11 (B2)
☎ 91 521 63 00
Mon.-Sat. 10am-2pm, 5-9pm.

Home to comic books, science-fiction and fantasy, the shelves here are lined with superheroes, Japanese mangas, Asterix, Tintin and erotic comic books. Metrópolis even stocks models from science fiction films, such as *Alien* and *Star Wars*, to build and paint, as well as books and screen plays of horror films.

La Tienda Verde

Calle Maudes, 23 and 38 (off map)
☎ 91 535 38
Mon.-Sat. 9.30am-2pm, 4.30-8.30pm.

If you're planning a walk in the magnificent nature reserves or mountains surrounding Madrid, this bookshop will provide you with the full details of the geographical and ecological aspects of your chosen destination. You'll find a multitude of books about nature, geology and astronomy as well as travel guides, charts and maps. It's definitely a shop for the ecologically-aware tourist.

8 y Medio

Martín de los Heros, 14 (A1)
☎ 91 559 58 51
Mon.-Sat. 4.30-9pm.

Housed in the basement of the cinema of the same name (which shows films in their original language), this shop is devoted to film fans and specialises in cinema-related graphic material, such as postcards, posters, and ephemera, both old and contemporary. If this whets your appetite, and you want to find out even more, go along to no. 23 in the same street. The 8 y Medio here

(Mon-Sat. 9.30am-1.30pm, 5-8pm) sells themed books, including screen plays, books on films and directors and biographies.

Desnivel
Plaza de Matute, 6 (B2)
☎ **91 369 47 27**
Mon.-Sat. 9.30am-9.30pm.

This shop in an attractive little square offers a vast choice of books for the keen adventurer on such topics as climbing, hiking and high-altitude mountaineering. You can consult books on every country in the world, and there are also a large number of videos, posters and maps for sale .

La Casa del Libro
Gran Vía, 29
☎ **91 521 21 13**
Mon.-Sat. 9.30am-9.30pm.

One of the biggest bookshops in Madrid, La Casa del Libro has all kinds of books on all kinds of subjects, including essays, travel and technology, as well as books for children. If you aren't lucky enough to find what you're looking for, they will be happy to order it for you.

Happy Books
Calle Goya, 55 (D1)
☎ **91 575 17 81**
Mon.-Sat. 9.30am-9.30pm.

You can find books on just about any subject here at unbeatable prices (from €0.60), including aviation, navigation, farming and, above all, a large number of books on Madrid.

Aliana
Calle General Varela, 6
(off map)
☎ **91 555 73 02**
Mon.-Fri. 10am-2pm,
5-8pm, Sat. 10am-2pm.

If you want to surprise your friends by cooking them a real Spanish dish, or if you like trying out recipes from all over the world, this is the place for you. Aliana sells hundreds of cookery books, including books on the history of cooking, new editions of old favourites and the latest popular titles.

FNAC
Calle Preciados, 28 (B2)
☎ **91 595 61 00**
Mon.-Sat. 11am-8pm.

A branch of the famous French-owned chain of bookshops, FNAC offers a wide range of books and magazines, including titles in English and other languages, and some more unusual services, such as theatre and concert reservations and film processing.

GOURMET DELIGHTS

Spain isn't particularly renowned for the finesse of its gourmet delicacies. The Spanish tend to regard mealtimes as an opportunity to spend time with friends and family rather than to satisfy their hunger. Yet you may be surprised at the great number of excellent culinary specialities that are available for you to discover. Have your shopping bags at the ready!

Viena Capellanes
Calle Génova, 4 and 25 (C1)
☎ 91 576 07 47
Every day 9am-9.30pm.

This chain of shops has had a long history in Madrid and there are branches all over the city. Not only is the shop window display enticing, but the specialities – almond pastries and biscuits – are absolutely delicious. You can eat them on the spot or take them away. The seasonal pastries and *turrón* are homemade, and the little sandwiches made from white bread are ideal for lunch on the hop. You'll need at least four of them to fill you up but there are over 30 different kinds to choose from (€0.55 each).

La Bodega del Alcalde
Galería ABC
Calle Serrano, 61 (C1)
☎ 91 575 19 16
Mon.-Sat. 10am-9.30pm.

This attractive little shop specialises in the wines of Priorato (a blend of Grenache, Cabernet Sauvignon and Shiraz grapes), and has an excellent selection. It also has a wide choice of Riojas and *Riberas del duero* on offer. If you don't want to load yourself down too much, you can arrange to have the wine sent anywhere in Europe.

Vela
Calle Santa Engracia, 42 (C1)
☎ 91 445 70 79
Mon.-Fri. 10.30am-2pm, 5.30-8.30pm, Sat. 10.30am-2pm.

Most of the wines sold in this family shop are Riojas and *Riberas del duero*, but other regions of Spain are also represented. In addition, you'll find liqueurs from all over the country. If you're buying Cava (a sparkling wine), don't look for the big names. They are set aside to promote lesser-known ones, such as *Recaredo* and *Monmarcal*.

La Dehesa
Calle Argensola, 21 (C1)
☎ 91 319 14 50
Mon.-Fri. 11am-2pm, Sat. 11am-2.30pm.

If you decide to take home some genuine Spanish olive oil, you'll find over 40 different kinds from all over the country in this shop. Do ask the assistants for advice, though, because the oils all have different flavours. The Andalusian oil is possibly the best. You'll be able to complete your shopping with Spanish and imported vinegars and cheese as well as tasty natural conserves and wine (expect to pay around €3-4 for a good bottle).

Niza

Calle Argensola, 24 (C1)
☎ **91 308 13 21**
**Every day 9.30am-2.30pm,
5-8.30pm.**

When you push open the door to *Niza*, with its large mirrors, marble counter and mouth-watering aroma, you'll think you've travelled back in time to a 19th-century confectioners and pastry shop. Do try the *roscon de Reyes* Christmas cake and the little tea biscuits – they're quite delicious.

Santa

Calle Serrano, 56 (C1)
☎ **91 576 86 46**
**Mon.-Sat. 10am-2pm,
5-8.30pm.**

They've done everything possible to entice you into this traditional chocolate-maker's (one of the last ones left in the city), from the welcoming, cosy decor and hushed atmosphere to the heady scent of the chocolate specialities that are displayed temptingly in glass cases. The shop is renowned for its

chocolate bouchées weighing over 50g/2oz each and *lena vieja*, a little Christmas log made entirely of chocolate. Diabetics haven't been forgotten either – there are even sweets made specially for them.

The Bomec

Calle Reina, 7 (B2)
☎ **91 531 16 15**
**Mon.-Sat. 11.30am-2pm,
5.30-9pm.**

There's nothing quite like a cup of tea after a hard day's sightseeing or shopping. The Bomec is one of the few tea merchants in Madrid where you can find such a wide selection of original flavours (including melon and pistachio), and some decorative accessories into the bargain.

BARGAIN CORNER

The Spanish love to dress well, and in designer clothes if possible. They are not inclined to spend a month's salary on a special outfit, though. If you like a bargain, you may be in luck. There are some great places to shop in the city, some of them relatively unknown, where you can shop to your heart's content, without feeling the guilt. Go ahead, it's a chance to spoil yourself.

El Almacen de loza
Calle Serrano, 218 (C1)
☎ 91 564 99 71
**Calle Nuñez de Balboa,
46 (D1)**
☎ 91 435 23 32
**Mon.-Fri. 10am-2pm,
5-8pm, Sat. 10am-2pm.**

If you'd like to lay your hands on some top-quality tableware, without breaking the bank, this is the place to come. Most of the items come from Portugal, but you'll also find Italian and French pieces. With dishes, plates (from €1.50), bowls, cups and teapots (around €6) on offer, you'll be spoilt for choice.

Carersa
Ronda de Toledo, 34 (A/B3)
☎ 91 467 49 43
**Mon.-Fri. 9am-2pm,
5-8.30pm, Sat. 9am-2pm.**

Carersa specialises in household electrical appliances, with items ranging from hair dryers to freezers. Because they've had a few knocks, they're sold with a 25% discount. If you're not sure what's wrong with them, ask before you buy – it may only be the packaging that's damaged – and remember to check that any item you purchase will be safe to use on your electrical supply when you get home.

MDM
**Calle Príncipe de Vergara,
120 (off map)**
☎ 91 564 63 02
Mon.-Sat. 9am-9pm.

The 2,000m²/21,500 sq ft of floor space are barely enough for these wholesalers to store the furniture they sell for your house, as well as your garden. The prices range from €60 for a pine deck chair to around €240 for a teak table imported from Borneo. Don't worry if you can't manage to fit an item of furniture in your weekend bag, you'll find all sorts of kitchen utensils and bathroom accessories as well.

Le Luva
**Calle Orense, 30
(off map)**
☎ 91 555 67 29
**Mon.-Fri. 9.30-2pm,
5-8.30pm.**

This relatively new shop sells designer clothes and accessories, including such names as Cerruti and Yves Saint Laurent. They may be secondhand or come from last year's collections, but one way or another you'll get a 50% reduction on the original price. You just have to rummage around to find the bargains. Expect to pay around €80 for a Versace outfit.

IL GRIFONE

Calle Lagasca, 62 (off map)
☎ **91 575 98 39**
**Mon.-Sat. 10.30am-2pm,
5-8.30pm.**

Il Grifone specialises in Italian designer clothes for both men and women, with last year's collections selling at unbeatable prices. You'll find stylish casual outfits, as well as fabulous evening dresses fit for an opening night at La Scala in Milan. This is luxury Italian fashion at affordable prices.

L'Habilleur

Plaza de Chueca, 8 (C1)
☎ **91 531 32 22**
Tue.-Sat. 11am-2pm, 5-9pm.

If you're keen on fashion, this is definitely the place to head for. Here you'll find reductions of up to 50 or 60% for labels such as Jean-Paul Gaultier, John Richmond, Antonio Fusco, Plein Sud and Dice Kayec, the Turkish designer who is currently in vogue. Expect to pay around €25-50 for one of her fabulous creations for evening wear. You can even buy your wedding dress here.

Marmota

Calle Mira el Rio Baja, 13 (A3)
☎ **91 467 24 52**
Mon.-Sat. 10.30am-2.30pm, 5.30-8.30pm.

If you have a soft spot for kitsch, you'll love this place. With the walls covered in an assortment of tins and bottles, the decor alone is worth coming for. As far as the clothes are concerned, Marmota has just about everything – secondhand clothes, surplus stock and even brand new 60s and 70s-style clothes that sell for €3 and upwards.

Rastrillo de Isabel García Tapia

Calle Juan del Risco, 24 (off map)
☎ **91 579 41 83**
Mon.-Fri. 10am-5.30pm, Sat. 10am-2pm.

This shop designs, sells and restores furniture and decorative objects for the home. But the most interesting things here are the ex-display models from fairs and shows. They're a real bargain, since you save between 40 and 50% on the normal prices.

Escuela de Divinos

Calle Zurbarán, 16 (C1)
☎ **91 308 28 16**
Mon.-Fri. 10am-2pm, 4.30-8pm, Sat. 10am-2pm.

This shop, run by the daughter of the famous designer Elena Benarroch (see page 87), sells women's clothes with well-known labels such as Bottega Venetta, and, of course, Elena Benarroch, at unbelievable prices (up to 50% reductions). The stock generally comprises unsold items from previous seasons.

Nightlife Practicalities

Madrid is renowned for its nightlife and for its incredible choice of bars, of all kinds and sizes. But don't miss out on its cultural life – the city is chock full of fascinating museums and theatres staging a dazzling variety of shows, plays, operas and *zarzuelas*. Don't hesitate – *vamos de juerga* – go have a blast!

WHERE TO GO FOR NIGHTLIFE

Madrid is like one big festival at night, and you'll find good bars in most of the districts. The bars in Chueca, the area frequented by the gay community, tend to be as trendy as their clients. You'll find a more mixed crowd around Plaza Santa Ana. In the daytime Lavapiés is mainly frequented by a quiet sort of clientele, who come to chat in the charming old bistros, but at night it attracts an 'underground' crowd, bent on seeking out the latest musical trends. The smart set and more conservative types tend to congregate in the Salamanca district and in the north of the city, while Malasaña offers 70s nostalgia to a fashionable crowd, but also attracts drug dealers.

BUDGETING

You'll be able to get into most bars free. You only have to pay for your drinks. To get into clubs and the more select bars, expect to pay around €18 per person, though this usually includes the price of a drink.

OPENING TIMES

If you like going to bed early you're in for a disappointment. There really isn't any atmosphere in the bars before midnight, and some don't really get going until around 1-1.30am. When it comes to clubs, don't think about arriving before 2 or 3am – they'll be empty any earlier.

WHERE TO FIND OUT ABOUT SHOWS

All the big national daily newspapers have an entertainment listings supplement, and usually a very good one, especially *Metropolis* – the supplement of *El Mundo*, which comes out on Fridays, and *El Espectador* – the supplement of *El País*, which comes out on Sundays. The *Guía del Ocio*, on sale at all kiosks and large bookshops, is also extremely useful, since it gives a complete picture of the cultural activities and events taking place in the city. For full information about the various programmes on offer, contact:

Información Turística y Cultural
☎ 91 540 40 10 or 901 300 600.

BOOKING THEATRE TICKETS

Throughout the year, and especially at festival time, Madrid offers a wide variety of shows and events. Some of the larger hotels will book seats for you, but most don't have this service. You can find out more from specialised agencies.

FNAC
☎ 91 595 61 00.

Crisol
☎ 91 575 06 40.

El Corte Inglés
☎ 91 532 18 00, 902 26 27 26 or 902 400 222.

Tel-Entradas
☎ 902 10 12 12.

Madrid Rock
☎ 91 521 02 39.

Caja Madrid
☎ 902 488 488
(seats for the Teatro Real).

LISTENING TO LIVE MUSIC

Some bars host live concerts all year round, notably the *Honky Tonk*, the *Clamores*, the *Café Central* and the *Solea* as well as many others (see page 10 and coloured section).

SAFETY

The districts with the most bars are packed with people. The atmosphere may seem pleasant enough but beware of pickpockets just the same, wherever you are. As with most large cities, it isn't unusual for foreigners to have their wallets or bags stolen. Malasaña is perhaps the least safe district and you also risk being accosted by drug dealers. There's also a scam that's becoming more and more common in Madrid – someone will puncture your tyre and then point it out to you. When you get out to check it, their accomplices steal everything on the seats.

WHAT TO WEAR

You don't have to dress up to the nines to do the rounds of the bars in Madrid. However, some clubs, such as the *Torero* and *Neil's* have a strictly-enforced dress code and don't let everyone in. If you want to spend the evening somewhere smart, leave the torn jeans and trainers behind.

NIGHTLIFE

It can't be said often enough that Madrid really comes to life at night. There are lively bars on every street corner, which can change their nature depending on the time of day. Even on weekday evenings, the discos and clubs don't empty until the early hours of the morning.

Tapas bars

Fiambres Licores
Calle Zorilla, 7 (C2)
☎ 91 32 48 12
Mon.-Fri. 9am-2pm, 5-8pm.

This establishment manages to fulfill the roles of both corner grocery store and local bistro. You can buy wine, liqueurs and fresh produce to take away, or have a *bocadillo* and a *vinito* (a sandwich and a glass of wine) at the counter. The walls are decorated with maps of Spain and old bottles.

Albur
Calle Manuela Malasaña, 15 (B1)
☎ 91 594 27 33
Every day noon-midnight.

The highlights of this small, unpretentious bar include *mejillones en salsa picante* (mussels in spicy sauce) and *morcilla de León* (blood sausage). Its a great place to come to enjoy tapas.

La Traditional
Calle Santo Tomé, 5 (C1)
☎ 91 310 15 03
Mon.-Sat. 11am-4.30pm, 6.30pm-midnight.

Recently renovated, this bar is renowned for its tapas. Try the *tortilla de patatas* (potato omelette), *ochetas de cordero* (lamb), *albondigas en salsa* (meatballs in sauce) and ham croquettes, all washed down with a draught beer or a glass of Rioja, *Ribera del duero* or *Rias baixas*. Find a table in one of the two dining rooms or soak up a bit of the atmosphere at the bar.

Tasca La Farmacía
Calle Diego de León, 9 (off map)
☎ 91 564 86 52
Mon.-Sat. 1-4pm, 9pm-midnight.

As its name suggests, this bar is housed in a former chemist's shop. The apothecary jars and phials lining the walls once contained medicinal herbs, and the azulejo tiles are adorned with portraits of biologists. There are plenty of tables, but you can also enjoy the delicious tapas at the bar. The house speciality is cod, prepared in five different ways. Don't worry if you don't like fish, you can always order the ham croquettes instead.

Taberna La Daniela
Calle General Pardiñas, 21 (off map)
☎ 91 575 23 29
Every day noon-4.30pm, 8-11.30pm.

A really typical Spanish tavern, decorated with azulejo tiles inside and out. If you sit at one of the tables this could be a good time to try the delicious *cocido*

madrileño (stew). If you prefer to remain at the bar, don't miss the tasty *empanadas*, the *tortilla paisana* (regional omelette) and the croquettes that are twice as big as you normally get. It's a popular place so it's best to book before coming if you want to be sure of a seat.

El Rincon de Goya

Calle Lagasca, 46 (off map)
☎ 91 576 38 89
Mon.-Fri. 8am-mid.,
Sat.-Sun. noon-4.30pm,
7pm-midnight.

Beautiful azulejo tiles and old posters set the tone in this bar, where the local regulars usually come fairly early. The ham or shrimp *croquetas de la abuela* ('grandmother's croquettes') are delicious. Try a plate of canapés, too (around €11).

Taberna El Buey

Calle General Pardiñas, 7 (off map)
☎ 91 578 11 54
Every day noon-4.30pm, 7.30pm-12.30am.

This bar, located opposite the restaurant of the same name, has a decor quite unlike the traditional tapas bar. The atmosphere here is modern and sophisticated. You can try the hot and cold canapés seated at a table or at the bar. The *solomillo a la pimienta* (peppered sirloin) and the *albondigas de buey* (beef meatballs) are particularly recommended.

El Barandal

Calle Independancia, 2 (A2)
☎ 91 541 11 33
Tue.-Sun. noon-4.30pm, 8pm-1am.

Bistro tables, warm orange walls, wood and wrought iron, as well as the music make this an ideal setting for an aperitif. If you're feeling hungry, you can try boar or salmon carpaccio followed by a salad. Don't miss the *queimada* which is served every Thursday at around midnight. Originally from Galicia, it's a mixture of brandy, coffee, lemon and sugar which is flambéed and drunk hot.

La Venencia

Calle Echegaray, 7 (B2)
☎ 91 429 73 13
Every day 1-3.30pm, 7.30pm-1.30am.

The years have left their mark on the walls of this bar in one of the liveliest parts of the capital. The menu is written directly on the old wooden bar. You can have all sorts of canapés as you make the acquaintance of the somewhat bohemian locals.

Tap-as

Calle Manuel Fernández y González, 17 (B2)
☎ 91 429 69 50
Mon.-Thu. and Sat. noon-5pm, 8pm-1am, Fri. 8pm-1am.

In this small bar, simply having a *vinito* and a *racion* becomes a pleasure for all five senses. The pretty little dining room, with its fine chairs and Victorian lamps, is particularly welcoming. Try the set meal of *tomates verdes fritos* (fried green tomatoes), *tapas del mar, del campo, de la nostalgía* (seafood, vegetable and nostalgic tapas), all prepared with great subtlety.

Teberna del Nuncio

Plaza Puerta Cerrada, 7 (A2)
☎ 91 364 56 29
Every day noon-4pm, 7.30pm-12.30am.

In a district with an impressive number of bars, this is just one among many. You can sit at a table or stand at the bar to sample hot and cold canapés, croquettes and salads.

La Salamandra

Calle Alfonso VI, 6 (A2)
Every day 1.30-4.30pm, 8.30pm-1am
Closed 15-31 Aug.

With its walls decorated with painted salamanders, this bar offers a good selection of wines (around sixty). If you like to experiment, the *solomillo de ternera con queso y frambuesa* (sirloin of veal with cheese and raspberries) and *solomillo de bellota* (sirloin of acorn-fed pork) are recommended.

Quiet bars

Café Unión

Calle Unión, 1 (A2)
☎ 91 542 55 63
Every day 7pm-2am.

Simple and pleasant, with a 19th-century air (even though it opened in 1981), this bar is an ideal place to come for a quiet chat over a cup of coffee. You may like to try a *café Unión*, which is the speciality of the house.

Teatriz

Calle Hermosilla, 15 (D1)
☎ 91 577 53 79
Every day 9pm-2am.

A few years ago the renowned designer, Philippe Starck, entirely renovated this old theatre. Although the bar is not very popular with the inhabitants of Madrid, it's really worth a visit. People tend to come here more for the decor of the rooms (the bar, the restaurant and the small lounges) than for the atmosphere. Aim for the tapas bar, which is just as good as the restaurant, and far more affordable. The toilets in the basement are an absolute must. You won't have seen anything like them before.

Cock

Calle Reina, 16 (B2)
☎ 91 532 28 26
Mon.-Sat. 7pm-3am.

This is a good place to come for a nightcap. The decor is sober and elegant, with high ceilings, antique furniture and a beautiful glass roof, and the cocktails are delicious.

More lively bars

La Sastrería

Calle Hortaleza, 74 (B1/2)
Every day 10-2am.

This former tailor's workshop has been converted into a bar and restaurant. At lunchtime, you may bump into a Spanish politician or two, while in the evenings it's frequented by *famosos* – the celebrities of the Madrid nightlife. Whatever time of day you come, try a slice of quiche, an *empanada* or a homemade dessert.

La Lupe

Calle Torrecilla del Leal, 12 (B3)
☎ 91 527 50 19
Every day 4pm-3am.

You can't claim to know Madrid if you haven't set foot in La Lupe.

Decorated with posters, on Sundays they host a mini-*rastro* (flea market), with old clothes and craft items on sale with the tapas. Thursday is theatre day and, starting recently, between 5 and 8pm, La Lupe is transformed into a tea room. The clients tend to be trendy and the atmosphere gets rather smoky.

La Bardemcilla

Calle Augusto Figueroa, 47 (B/C1)
☎ 91 521 42 56
Mon.-Fri. noon-4.30pm, midnight-2am,
Sat. midnight-2am.

With parquet flooring and soft lighting, this bar has a very welcoming atmosphere. The decor is based around the cinema and each dish bears the name of a film in which the owners have acted. A restaurant at lunchtime, it becomes a bar in the evening.

El Viso

Calle Juan Bravo, 31 (off map)
☎ 91 562 23 79
Mon.-Sat. 9pm-4am.

This establishment is arranged on three floors, each with a different atmosphere. On the top floor, you'll find a billiard table and a quiet setting. Downstairs, you'll find a club atmosphere with deafening music. Things don't really get going before 12.30am at the earliest.

Dejate Besar

Calle Hermanos Bécquer, 10 (off map)
☎ 91 562 54 85
Tue.-Sat. 10pm-3am.

Literally translated, the name means 'Let yourself be kissed', an original name taken from a Spanish radio show that broadcasts the latest music. The decor could be straight out of a David Lynch film, with red curtains, leopardskin-covered columns, wrought-iron wall lamps, mirror balls and even a fur-lined cloakroom. People of all ages come here, but not before 1am.

Torero

Calle Cruz, 26 (B2)
☎ 91 523 11 29
Every day 11pm-5.30am.

Torero is currently very much in vogue. They play Spanish and Latino music (flamenco and salsa) on the first floor, where you can see the head of the bull that killed the famous *torero*

Manolete rather gruesomely adorning the wall. Funk and house fans will prefer to stay downstairs. You won't find many people arriving much before 1-1.30am.

Cabaret, jazz and shows

Cafe Central

Plaza del Angel, 10 (B2)
☎ 91 369 41 43
Mon.-Sun. 4pm-3am.

Cafe Central is a mecca for jazz fans. Concerts are staged here every week, and you can get a

monthly programme of the events at the bar. The café is packed in the evening, but the retro decor makes it a very pleasant place to relax in the afternoon.

Clamores Jazz

Calle Alburquerque, 1 (B1)
☎ 91 445 79 38
Every day 7pm-3am.

This is the very heart of Madrid's jazz scene. There are high-quality concerts held every week, and blues, salsa and country can also be heard here.

Honky Tonk

Calle Covarrubias, 24 (B1)
☎ 91 445 68 86
Every day 10pm-5.30am.

Honky Tonk is one of Madrid's great classic venues. A favourite with both rock and pop fans alike, besides the popular live concerts they also stage plays and magic shows. Performances in the basement start at 3am.

Cafe del Foro

Calle San Andrés, 38 (B1)
☎ 91 445 37 52
Every day 7pm-3am.

You're sure to fall under the spell of this charming café. With its walls lined with recon-structions of old shops, the largest room resembles a village square. The other room is decorated with old posters. There are performances in the middle of the 'village square' every evening, at around 11pm on weekdays and 9pm on Sundays.

Flamenco and dance clubs

Almonte

Calle Juan Bravo, 35
(off map)
☎ 91 563 25 04
Every day 9pm–5am.

A large bar, decorated in the style of the Seville *feria*, with azulejo tiles and unusual bullfighting photos. If you've ever swayed to the strains of the Gipsy Kings, this is your chance to really put

your heart into it. People come here to dance or to watch others dance, with sevillanas, rumbas and salsas featuring on the programme. Groups perform from Sunday to Wednesday, at 1am and 3am.

Cafe de Chinitas

Calle Torija, 7 (A1)
☎ 91 547 15 02
Mon.–Sat. 9pm–3am.

You can dine while watching the show (around €57) at this restaurant, housed in a 17th-century palace. If you don't fancy a meal, it's possible just to have a drink during the midnight performance (€26). The show is renowned and includes performances by the great names of flamenco, such as Enrique Morente and Manuela Vargas. You can also admire the fine collection of *mantónes de Manilla* on display.

Peña Chaquetón

Calle Canarias, 39
(basement – off map)
☎ 91 671 27 77
Fri. around 11.30pm.

Real afficionados of flamenco and bullfighting congregate in this club, reserved for *cante flamenco* purists. It isn't possible to have a meal here and there isn't any dancing either, just a bar that serves drinks while you listen to a *cantaor* singing

songs of love and betrayal, in the traditional way without the aid of a microphone.

Casa PATAS

Calle Cañizares, 10 (B2)
☎ 91 369 04 96
Mon.–Sat. noon–5pm, 8pm–2am.

This is both a bar and a *tablao flamenco*. Renowned for the variety of its programmes, it's here that the flamenco fans of Madrid often come to witness performances by *cantaores* and *bailaores* on weekday evenings at around 11pm (midnight on Saturdays).

Clubbing

Nells

Calle López de Hoyos, 25
(off map)
☎ 91 562 49 54
Tue.–Sat. midnight–6am
Entry charge.

Currently very fashionable, this place is more like a private club than a disco. It's frequented mainly by the *gente guapa* of Madrid – attractive girls and smart thirty-something men. It draws record crowds at the weekend.

Joy Eslava

Calle Arenal, 11 (B2)
Every day 11pm–6am
Entry charge.

A typical Madrid bar housed in a former theatre, with a decor dating from the 19th century.

The original three galleries of the theatre have a fantastic view of the dance floor. You meet a very cosmopolitan crowd here, from artists and intellectuals to jet-setters. Prince Felipe, the most eligible bachelor in Spain, is even said to come here from time to time. There's a cabaret show at around 2am from Thursday to Sunday and things don't hot up until well after midnight.

Empire

Paseo de Recoletos, 16 (C1/2)
☎ 91 431 54 27
Every day 11pm-5am
Entry charge.

Once the city's third-largest theatre, this venue has been turned into a nightclub with a very charming decor. With its five bars, capacity for seven hundred people and trendy, varied clientele, *tiene mucha marcha* (it's got loads of atmosphere), as the Spanish say.

Pachá

Calle Barceló, 1 (B1)
☎ 91 447 01 28
Wed.-Sat. 12.30-5am
Entry charge.

Another converted theatre, Pachá sets the standard for the *Madrileño marcha*. It's frequented by a mixed crowd of students, businessmen and *famosos* (the Spanish jet-set) as well as a gay crowd and drag queens, who all get down to the throbbing dance music.

Clubbing through the early hours

Underground

Pasaje Martín de los Heros, 14 (A1)
☎ 91 388 99 72
Thu.-Sun. 5-10.30am
Entry charge.

Even at 5 o'clock in the morning the party's far from over, at least as far as dedicated clubbers are concerned. This place can hold up to 1,600 people and it's packed at the weekend, with loud house music and a very mixed clientele.

Roxy

Calle Orense, 14 (off map)
☎ 92 904 35 59
Sat.-Sun. 5-11am.

A trendy audience made up of artists and showbiz personalities meets regularly in this lively place to carry on partying into the morning. It's an experience you won't want to miss.

Classical music and theatre

Auditorium Nacional de Mùsica

Calle Principe de Vergara, 146 (off map)
☎ 91 337 01 00
Information every day.
8am-10pm.

Inaugurated in 1988, the Auditorium Nacional de Mùsica is the place to come to listen to classical music in Madrid. The Auditorium has two halls, one dedicated to chamber music and the other for symphonic music. The largest, highly-renowned international orchestras perform here on a regular basis, as well as the Spanish national orchestra and choir.

Teatro de la Zarzuela

Calle Jovellanos, 4 (B2)
☎ 91 524 54 00
Box office open every day noon-6pm

If you're in the city in July or November, don't miss the *zarzuela* – Madrid's own form of comic operetta. This theatre seems tailor-made for them but it also stages operas, ballets (with the Spanish national ballet) and contemporary dance (with the national dance company).

More handy words and phrases

Don't assume that everyone in Madrid will speak English. Although multilingual people are often employed in places that deal with tourists, this is by no means the norm. More Handy Words and Phrases can be found on the back flap of the cover.

USEFUL EXPRESSIONS

Good morning
buenos días

Good afternoon
Buenas tardes

Good evening
Buenas noches

Can you speak more slowly, please?
¿Puede hablar mas despacio, por favor?

Do you understand?
¿Me entiende?

I am sorry
Lo siento/ Disculpe

Is it possible...?
¿Sería posible....?

I want…
Quiero…

How?
¿Cómo?

What is your name?
¿Como se llama?

My name is …
Me llamo …

Free (no charge)
Gratis

Toilets/WC
Baño or aseos

No smoking
No fumar

Here/there
Aqui/allá

Early/late
Temprano/tarde

Slow
Lento

Fast
Rápido

Another
Otra vez

Before
Antes

After
Dopo

During
Durante

Near
Cerca

Now
Ahora

Up there
Arriba

IN THE RESTAURANT

Meal
Comida

The wine list
La lista de vinos

What is the dish of the day?
¿Cual es el plato del dia?

What is the house specialty?
¿Cual es la especialidad de la casa?

Tip
Propina

Plate
Plato

DRINKS

Still/sparkling
Sin gas/con gas

Red/white
Tinto/blanco

Sparkling wine
Cava

Sherry
Jerez

Lemonade
Limonada

Orange juice
Zumo de naranja

Tea
Té

SUNDRIES

Sugar
Azúcar

Salt
Sal

Pepper
Pimienta

Mustard
Mostaza

Sauce
Salsa

Spicy
Picante

Oil
Aceite

Vinegar
Vinagre

Sandwich
Bocadillo

Omelette
Tortilla

Egg
Huevo

Rice
Arroz

Fruit
Fruta

MEAT AND FISH

Meat
Carne

Ham
Jamón

Sausage
Chorizo/embutido

Blood sausage
Morcilla

Shrimp
Langostino/gamba

Squid
Pulpo

Oysters
Ostras

NUMBERS

1 uno
2 dos
3 tres
4 cuatro
5 cinco
6 seis
7 siete
8 ocho
9 nueve
10 diez
11 once
12 doce
13 trece
14 catorce
15 quince
16 dieciseis
17 diecisiete
18 dieciocho
19 diecinueve
20 veinte
21 veintiuno
22 veintidos
30 treinta
40 cuarenta
50 cincuenta
60 sesenta
70 setenta
80 ochenta
90 noventa
100 cien
1,000 mil
2,000 dosmil
5,000 cincomil
1,000,000 un millon

first
primero/a
second
segundo/a
third
tercero/a
fourth
cuarto/a
fifth
quinto/a

TIMES AND DATES

Yesterday
Ayer
Today
Hoy

Tomorrow
Mañana
One minute
Un minuto
One hour
Una hora
Half an hour
Media hora
Quarter of an hour
Cuarto de hora
It is midnight
Es medianoche
It's noon
Es mediodia
It's one o'clock
Es la una
See you tomorrow
Hasta mañana
What time is it?
¿Qué hora es?
Watch
Reloj

IN THE TOWN

News-stand
Kiosco de revistas
Bookshop
Librería
What time does it open/close?
¿A qué hora abre/cierra?
Straight on
Todo recto
Right/left
Derecha/izquierda
At the end of
Al final de
Next to
Al lado de
Opposite
Frente a
Up/down
Arriba/abajo
Above/below
Sobre/debajo
Entrance
Entrada
Exit
Salida
I would like to go
Quisiera ir

Timetable
Horario
By plane/train/car
Por avión/tren/coche
Airport
Aeropuerto
Do I need to change?
¿Debo cambiar de platforma?
What platform does it leave from?
¿De qué plataforma sale?
Bicycle
Bicicleta
On foot
A pie
Bend
Vuelta

SHOPPING

Size
Talla
Small
Pequeña
Medium
Mediana
Large
Grande
Bigger
Más grande
Smaller
Más pequeño
In another colour
De otro color
It's too expensive
Es demasiado caro
Big/little
Grande/pequeño
Money
Dinero
Price
Precio
I would like to buy
Quisiera comprar
Where can I find...?
¿Dónde puedo encontrar...?
Sale goods
Rebajas
Secondhand objects
Objetos usados/de segunda mano

Conversion tables for clothes shopping

Women's sizes

Shirts/dresses

U.K	U.S.A	EUROPE
8	6	36
10	8	38
12	10	40
14	12	42
16	14	44
18	16	46

Sweaters

U.K	U.S.A	EUROPE
8	6	44
10	8	46
12	10	48
14	12	50
16	14	52

Shoes

U.K	U.S.A	EUROPE
3	5	36
4	6	37
5	7	38
6	8	39
7	9	40
8	10	41

Men's sizes

Shirts

U.K	U.S.A	EUROPE
14	14	36
$14^{1/2}$	$14^{1/2}$	37
15	15	38
$15^{1/2}$	$15^{1/2}$	39
16	16	41
$16^{1/2}$	$16^{1/2}$	42
17	17	43
$17^{1/2}$	$17^{1/2}$	44
18	18	46

Suits

U.K	U.S.A	EUROPE
36	36	46
38	38	48
40	40	50
42	42	52
44	44	54
46	46	56

Shoes

U.K	U.S.A	EUROPE
6	8	39
7	9	40
8	10	41
9	10.5	42
10	11	43
11	12	44
12	13	45

More useful conversions

1 centimetre	0.39 inches	1 inch	2.54 centimetres
1 metre	1.09 yards	1 yard	0.91 metres
1 kilometre	0.62 miles	1 mile	1.61 kilometres
1 litre	1.76 pints	1 pint	0.57 litres
1 gram	0.035 ounces	1 ounce	28.35 grams
1 kilogram	2.2 pounds	1 pound	0.45 kilograms

This guide was written by **Mathilde Biscay** and **Delphine Desveaux**
Translated and edited by **Margaret Rocques**
Series editor **Liz Coghill**
Additional research and assistance: **Caroline Boissy**, **Sophie Janssens**,
Aurélie Joiris, **Anne-Gaëlle Moutarde** and **Christine Bell**

We have done our best to ensure the accuracy of the information contained in this guide.
However, addresses, phone numbers, opening times etc. inevitably do change from time
to time, so if you find a discrepancy please do let us know. You can contact us at the
address below.

Hachette Travel Guides provide independent advice. The authors and compilers do not accept
any remuneration for the inclusion of any addresses in these guides.

Please note that we cannot accept any responsibility for any loss, injury or inconvenience
sustained by anyone as a result of any information or advice contained in this guide.

Photo acknowledgements
Inside pages
All the photographs in this book were taken by **Nicolas Edwige**, except for those on the
following pages:

Jacques Debru: p. 11 (t. l.), p. 15 (b. r.), p. 20 (t. l.; t. r.), p. 29 (t. l.)
Laurent Parrault: p. 27 (b. l.), p. 31 (c. l.; b. r.)
Photothèque Hachette: p. 12 (c. l.), p. 22 (c .l.), p. 23 (t. r.), p. 24 (b. c.),
Spanish Tourist Office p. 15 (t. l.), © F. Ontañón p. 22 (t. r.), p. 22 (b. r.), p. 23 (b. r.),
© A. Puente Briales p. 23 (c. l.), © N. Müller p. 25 (t. r.), p. 37 (t. c.; c. r), © F. Ontañón
p. 41 (t. l.) and p. 69 (b. l.), © Miguel Otero p. 53 (c. l.) and p. 56 (b.)

Front cover
All the photographs were taken by **Nicolas Edwige**, except for::
Stock Image: c. t. (figure); **Lee Page, Tony Stone Images**: c. r. (figure) and c. b. (figures).

Back cover
Nicolas Edwige

Illustrations Virginia Puim
Cartography © Hachette Tourisme

First published in the United Kingdom in 2000 by Hachette UK. Reprinted 2003

© English Translation, revised and adapted, Hachette UK 2000
© Hachette Livre (Hachette Tourisme) 1999

Distributed in the United States of America by Sterling Publishing Co., Inc.
387 Park Avenue South, New York, NY 10016-8810

A CIP catalogue for this book is available from the British Library

ISBN 1 84202 095 1

Hachette Travel Guides, c/o Philip's, 2-4 Heron Quays, London E14 4JP

Printed and bound in Slovenia

If you're staying on and would like to try some new places, the following pages give you a wide choice of restaurants, clubs and bars, listed by district with addresses.

Don't forget, you'll need to book well in advance for the more fashionable restaurants as well as the most prestigious establishments. For more information, (see pages 70–71). All prices given are a guideline only. Enjoy your stay!

STAYING ON
A LITTLE LONGER

Whether you want a quick snack, a romantic dinner for two or an enjoyable meal with friends and family, you'll find Madrid caters for all occasions.

La Latina

El Lando
Plaza Gabriel Miró, 8
☎ 91 366 76 81
Mon.-Sat. 1.30-4pm,
9pm-12.30am, closed
Sun. and holidays
Around €30.
The smart, trendy crowd who used to frequent Casa Lucio now come to this restaurant, which serves excellent traditional cuisine.

El Schotis
Calle Cava Baja, 11
☎ 91 365 32 30
Mon.-Sat. 1-4.30pm,
8.30pm-12.30am,
Sun. 1-4.30pm
Around €25.
An old inn that's one of many similar establishments in the district. Fine frescoes depicting scenes of the Madrid of yesteryear decorate the walls. The traditional cuisine and high-quality service make it a good place to come for lunch or dinner.

Nuevos Ministerios

Gaztelupe
Calle Comandante Zorita, 32
☎ 91 534 90 28
Mon.-Sat. 1.30-4pm,
8.30pm-midnight
Around €30.
Basque specialities feature high on the menu of this large restaurant. The bright, pleasant decor includes green and white checked tablecloths with ceramic plates adorning the walls. The friendly waiters and high-quality traditional Basque cuisine will make you glad you came. Try the ventresca de Atún (the tenderest cut of tuna) and marmitako (tuna soup with potatoes and green peppers). The portions are certainly very generous.

Cuzco

La Broche
Calle Doctor Fleming, 36
☎ 91 457 99 60
Mon.-Fri. 1.30-3.30pm,
9-11.30pm,
Sat. 9-11.30pm,
cosed Easter week and Aug.
Around €39.
This restaurant is for gourmets who are fond of creative cuisine. There's nothing traditional on the menu here, everything's straight out of the imagination of the Catalan host, Sergi Arola. The decor is very simple and the atmosphere is nothing special, but the food is very exciting and imaginative.

Rubén Darío

Las Pocholas
Calle Fortuny, 47
☎ 91 308 01 07
Mon.-Fri. 1.30-4pm,
9pm-midnight,
Sat. 9pm-midnight.
An Art Deco-style restaurant serving traditional cuisine. There are several small private rooms. The duck's liver (around €17) and beef solomillo (sirloin) (around €17) are excellent.

El Viejo León
Calle Alfonso X, 6
☎ 91 310 06 83
Mon.-Fri. 9am-5pm,
8pm-1am,
Sat. 8pm-1am
Around €30.
A small, intimate restaurant with a rather old-fashioned decor and few tables. People come here for the French bistro-style cuisine.

Chueca

Kikuyu
Calle Bárbara de Braganza, 4
☎ 91 319 66 11
Mon.-Sat. 2-4pm,
9pm-midnight,
closed holidays
Around €30.
One of the restaurants currently in vogue, Kikuyu has a refined, modern decor and soft lighting. The small indoor patio is covered in green plants and you'll be served Mediterranean cuisine that's light and tasty.

Qoricancha
Calle Augusto Figueroa, 32
☎ 91 522 55 99
Mon.-Sat. 1-4pm,
9pm-midnight
Around €30.
If you aren't familiar with Peruvian cuisine, this is a chance to discover some of the various specialities while admiring the latest exhbition of sculptures or paintings. The works on display are also for sale.

Zara
Calle Infantas, 5
☎ 91 532 20 74
Mon.-Fri. 1-4.30pm,
8-11.30pm
Around €18.
Inés Llanos and Pepe Martínez left Cuba in 1960 to come and open a restaurant in the centre of Madrid. With its rustic decor and Latino music, it's become one of the most popular places to dine in the city. It serves typically Cuban dishes at very reasonable prices and the best daiquiris for miles.

La Castafiore
Calle Barquillo, 30
☎ 91 532 21 00
Mon.-Sat. 2-4.30pm,
9pm-1am
Around €33-36.
If you're an opera lover, you can indulge your passion here – the waiters sing arias during the meal. However, conversation is difficult, if not impossible. If you've got a lot to say, or you're looking for a quiet dinner for two, it may be better to try somewhere else.

Prado

Balzac
Calle Moreto, 7
☎ 91 420 01 77 or
91 420 06 13
Mon.-Sat. 1.30-4pm,
9-11.30pm, closed
holidays and Aug.
Around €33-36.
This is one of the few smart restaurants in this residential district. Because of the number of large companies in the area, the place is generally full up at lunchtime with executives and office workers, but it's quieter in the evening. The simple decor is rather ordinary, but the menu

includes Mediterranean and Provençal specialities and some very tasty desserts. Don't forget to consult the excellent wine list for a suitable sweet wine to go with them.

Banco de España

La Vaca Verónica
Calle Moratín, 38
☎ 91 429 78 27
Mon.-Fri. 1.30-4pm,
9pm-midnight,
Sat. 9pm-midnight
Around €25.
A restaurant offering the decor of a turn-of-the-century Madrileño appartment, with soft lighting and serving excellent Argentinian meat dishes, as well as a variety of other good things to try.

Casa Manolo
Calle Jovellanos,7
☎ 91 521 45 16
Mon.-Sat. 1-4.30,
8.30pm-midnight,
closed Aug.
Around €13-15.
This old bistro, dating from 1896, was frequented by politicians and artists in the early 20th century. Since then, it's as if time has stood still here and nothing much has changed. You'll find bistro tables, slot machines, good traditional cuisine and old regulars, who like to drop in for a chat now and again.

Errota Zar
Calle Jovellanos, 3
(1st floor)
☎ 91 531 25 64
Mon.-Sat. 1-4pm,
9pm-midnight, closed
Sun. and Easter week
Around €30-33.
Located opposite the Teatro de la Zarzuela, this house, decorated in a traditional style, is also the restaurant of Euskal Etxea, the Basque Centre. It's renowned for its red meat and homemade desserts, such as cuajada, a type of yoghurt made with milk curds. The menus are written in Basque and Castilian.

Paradís Madrid
Calle Marqués de Cuba, 14
☎ 91 429 73 03
Mon.-Fri. 1.30-4pm,
9pm-midnight,
Sat. 9pm-midnight,
closed Easter week
and Aug.
Around €33.
This restaurant, frequented by businessmen, has a simple decor. Their Catalan cuisine is renowned and you can wash it down with a wide choice of wines, most of which can be ordered by the glass. Its originality lies in the little bar-cum-shop in the entrance where wine and a very wide choice of oils and top-quality vinegars are on offer.

Terra Mundi
Calle Lope de Vega, 32
☎ 91 429 52 80
Mon. 1-4.30pm,
Tue.-Sun. 1-4.30pm,
8.30pm-midnight
Around €18 à la carte,
set meal €7.50.
A restaurant in the style of a Galician country house. With pale wood rooms, green and white checked tablecloths and still life paintings on the walls, it has a holiday air about it. There's also a little shop selling homemade preserves.

Palacio Real

La Esquina del Real
Calle Amnistia, 2
☎ 91 559 43 09
Mon.-Fri. 2-4pm,
9-11.30pm,
Sat. 8pm-midnight
Around €30.
This very welcoming restaurant is housed in a 17th-century building a stone's throw from the Teatro Real. The chef is French, as is the cuisine.

Cuatro Caminos

Taverna San Mamés
Calle Bravo Murillo, 88
☎ 91 534 50 65
Mon.-Fri. 1.30-4pm,
8.30-11.30pm,
Sat. 2.30-4pm,
closed holidays and Aug.
Around €30.
It may not be in a particularly good district, but this picturesque tavern is worth coming for. The walls of the two tiny rooms are lined with azulejo tiles, with a few tables for regulars. The cuisine is delicious (regional specialities or fresh liver) and the service is very friendly.

RESTAURANTS

Lista

El Pescador
Calle José Ortega y
Gasset, 75
☎ 91 402 12 90
Mon.-Sat. 1-4pm,
8.30pm-midnight
Around €39.
*One of the best fish restaurants
in Madrid, El Pescador has a very
rustic decor, with fishermen's
nets hanging from the ceiling
and red and white checked
cloths on the tables. The
lenguado evaristo (large sole)
is well worth trying.*

Alonso Cano

Paulino
Calle Alonso Cano, 34
☎ 91 441 87 37
Mon.-Sat. 1.30-4pm,
9-11.30pm
Around €25.
*Gourmet cuisine at fairly
reasonable prices. Most of the
dishes are inspired by recipes
of the great chefs. It's a bit of a
squeeze, but it doesn't matter.
You come here for the solomillo
al vino tinto con foie (sirloin in
red wine with liver) and tarta de
chocolate (chocolate tart).*

Tetuán

**El Viejo Almacén
de Buenos Aires**
Calle Villaamil, 277
☎ 91 316 13. 17
Tue.-Sat. 1-4pm,
9pm-12.30am
Around €30.
*Famed for the tender red meat
it serves and the tango music
played as you dine, this
restaurant stages performances
by singers and dancers, and you
can join them on stage if you
feel like it.*

Paseo de la Florida

Casa Mingo
Paseo de la Florida, 2
☎ 91 547 79 18
Every day 11am-midnight
Around €9.
*Just opposite the Ermita de
San Antonio de la Florida, where
you can admire frescoes by
Goya, you'll find one of Madrid's
legendary spots. In winter you
dine in a vast wood-panelled
room, while in summer the
terrace is packed. But whatever
the season, you can be sure of
the menu – delicious grilled
chicken, empanadas and salad,
helped down with a glass of
cider.*

RESTAURANTS

Bars

La Latina

La Soleá
Calle Cava Baja, 34
☎ 91 365 52 64
Mon.-Sat. 10pm-6am.
This is a really great place. The two rooms decorated with azulejo tiles on the ground floor are set aside for flamenco music. The bar starts to get crowded by about 10.30pm, and amateur as well as professional cantaores, accompanied by guitarists, begin their repertoire. The lovely old vaulted cellar in the basement, however, is the setting for some excellent jazz concerts. On Mondays any musicians are invited onto the stage to join in the jam session.

Atocha

La Vieja Estación
Estación de Atocha
(corner of Avenida de la Ciudad de Barcelona)
All summer 10pm-4am.
If you want to find out what Madrid nights are really like, this terrace in the old Estación de Atocha will give you a good idea. It opened four years ago and is packed at the weekend in the summer months. There are bars with dance floors, karaoke, and tables in old train carriages. Just don't expect it to warm up too early.

Huertas

La Fontanería
Calle Hueras, 38
☎ 91 369 94 04
Every day 7pm-3am.
This bar was once a plumber's merchants, which explains the idea behind the decor – there are taps and pipes galore. It's a very fashionable place and is always crowded.

Alonsó Martinez

Barnon
Calle Santa Engracia, 17
☎ 91 447 38 87
Every day 10pm-5am.
If you're a football fan and would like to meet members of the Real Madrid team, this is the place to come. It's currently very fashionable, or famoso, and is
popular with beautiful girls and members of the paparazzi looking for a scoop.

Café de Los Artistas
Plaza Colón
Every day 1-4pm, 8.30pm-1am.
This café, just below the central reservation of Plaza Colón, is also a restaurant. With a decor that's a mix of the modern and the Baroque, it's a pleasant place to come for a drink. It's absolutely packed at the weekend.

La Palma 62
Calle Palma, 62
☎ 91 522 50 31
Every day 4pm-3am.
The decor here is a bit grunge and a bit alternative, with a strong Moroccan flavour. You sit on mats and chat while you drink your herb tea. They also stage live concerts, but it's a bit of a challenge to find out exactly when they're on. After opening three years ago, the bar is rapidly becoming one of the district's classics.

Chueca

Kingston's
Calle Barquillo, 29
91 521 15 68
Every day 10pm-3am.
The most important thing here is the music, whether it's funk, soul or reggae. You may even be lucky enough to bump into cult film director Pedro Almodóvar.

Liquid
Calle Barquillo, 8
Every day 10pm-2.30am.
Liquid is an original combination of café and video bar, where you can watch the latest clips on various screens. The clientele is fairly mixed.

Goya

Geographic Club
Calle Alcalá, 141
☎ 91 578 08 62
Every day 12.30pm-1am.
With a decor inspired by Jules Vernes' Around the World in 80 Days, this is currently one of the most original places in Madrid. You'll be left dreaming of travel and adventure.

Nightclubs

Salamanca

Gabana 1800
Calle Velázquez, 6
☎ 91 576 06 86
Wed.-Sat. midnight-5am.
Entry charge €30, including a drink.
Since it opened over a year ago, this club, with its designer decor has become very fashionable. Playing disco music and latest hits, it attracts fashionable young women and Madrid's trendy jet-set. The dress code is smart and elegant.

Cuzco

Monet
Calle Padre Damián, 23
☎ 91 448 19 19
Mon.-Thu. 11.30pm-5.30am, Fri.-Sat. midnight-6am
Entry charge €30.
This disco inside the NH chain's Hotel Eurobuilding is very fashionable at the moment. It's often used for marketing or launching new products. If you like sevillanas, don't miss the noches rocieras spot at midnight on Tuesdays.

Sol

Katmandú
Calle Señores de Luzón, 3
☎ 91 364 42 01
Thu.-Sat. midnight-5am.
A classic nightclub, where you can dance the night away to the beat of Afro and funk.

BARS

Excursions in the surrounding area

If you're staying in Madrid a little longer, some of the towns in the surrounding area are really worth a visit.

TOLEDO

Toledo, which lies 70km/44 miles from Madrid, has been declared a World Heritage Site by UNESCO. Its very rich history makes it the epitome of a museum city. It was the capital of Spain in 554, and the Jewish, Muslim and Christian religions existed side by side here peacefully for five centuries. You'll be spoilt for choice for interesting places to visit, but make sure you check the opening times – the monuments are often closed between 1 and 4pm. Don't miss the cathedral, which was built between 1227 and 1493.
The works by El Greco and Van Dyck housed in the sacristy alone are worth the trip.
Also pay a visit to El Greco's house, the Iglesia Santo Tome, home to his famous painting El Entiero del Conde de Orgaz (The burial of the Count of Orgaz), and the Sinagoga de Santa María la Blanca, that was turned into a church in the 15th century. It has been carefully restored and is now close to its original beauty.

GETTING THERE
You can get to Toledo by train from Estación de Atocha, departing every hour, or by bus from Estación Sur de Autobus (Calle Méndez Alvaro ☎ 91 468 42 00).

WHERE TO EAT
A good place to have lunch is La Casa Aurelio (Calle Sinagoga, 6, ☎ 92 522 20 97), which serves good traditional cuisine, or try one of the terraces of Plaza Zocodover, if you prefer.

ARANJUEZ

At the meeting point of the Tagus and Jarama rivers, and lying 47km (29 miles) from Madrid, Aranjuez was the summer residence of the kings at the time of the Habsburg and Bourbon dynasties. It not only attracted kings but also inspired the famous Spanish composer Joaquín Rodrigo to write his Concerto de Aranjuez.
Renowned for centuries for its strawberries and asparagus, the town is currently a favourite refuge of Madrileños in search of fresh air and greenery.

The Palacio Real (Wed.-Sun. 10am-5.15pm), the beautiful royal palace, was built by Juan de Herrera, the architect of El Escorial, in the 18th century and was later altered by Felipe IV and Carlos II. Look out for the smoking room (inspired by one of the rooms in the Alhambra in Granada), the Flemish tapestries, the French clocks and, above all, the Porcelain Room. Go for a walk in the Jardín del Príncipe (Jun.-Sep. 8.30am-8.30pm, Oct.-May 8am-6.30pm), where you'll see the Casa del Labrador (labourer's cottage – 10am-6.15pm), a decorative pavilion built by Carlos IV which contains marvellous silk embroideries depicting Madrid. The Casa de Marinos (sailor's house – 10am-6.15pm), houses royal boats.

GETTING THERE
You can get to Aranjuez by train from Estación de Atocha, departing every 30 minutes for a 45-minute journey, or by bus from Estación Sur de Autobus (Calle Méndez Alvaro ☎ 91 468 42 00), with a journey lasting 60 minutes.

From 13 May to 30 September, you can take the 'tren de la fresa' (strawberry train), an exact replica of the second steam locomotive that ran between Madrid and Aranjuez last century to bring strawberries to the capital. It departs from Estación de Atocha at 10am on Sat. and Sun., returning at 6.30pm, except in August. The ticket price includes entrance to the sites. For further information call ☎ 90 222 88 22.

WHERE TO EAT
You can have lunch at La Casa San Pablo (Calle Almídar, 42 ☎ 91 891 14 51), a restaurant renowned for specialities such as suckling pig and Labrador pheasant.

CHINCHÓN

This charming little village, with its beautiful medieval square, lies 50km (31 miles) from Madrid and 20km (12 miles) from Aranjuez. The Madrileños often come here for lunch on Sundays. Wandering through the narrow streets, looking round the traditional ceramic shops and having an aperitif in the square is a very pleasant way to spend the day. Chinchón's locally produced anis is renowned.

GETTING THERE
You can get to Chinchón by La Veloz bus, departing from Avenida del Mediterraneo, 49, ☎ 91 409 76 04.

WHERE TO EAT
For a delicious lunch try Le Mesón Cuevas de Vinos (Calle Benito Hortelano, 13 ☎ 91 894 02 06). Housed in former wine cellars, Le Mesón serves such delicacies as suckling pig, pork chops, etc.

SEGOVIA

Segovia, a charming old city perched high on a rocky outcrop 86km (54 miles) from Madrid, is a UNESCO World Heritage Site. The aqueduct that still crosses it to this day was built under the Roman Emperor Augustus. Take the time to stroll through the streets and discover the Romanesque churches of San Esteban and San Martín, with its arcades and Mudéjar tower. The Renaissance-style palace in Plaza San Martín is also worth a look. The cathedral, dating from 1525, is in the high city. An elegant and graceful building, it houses a collection of 17th-tapestries. The Alcázar, of course, mustn't be missed. Rising above the rocky crags, this fairy-tale castle contains some ornately decorated rooms and a museum of weaponry.

HOW TO GET THERE

You can get to Segovia by train from Estación de Atocha or Chamartín, or by Empresa la Sepuvedana bus (Paseo de la Florida, 11 ☎ 91 530 48 00).

WHERE TO EAT

There are a number of taverns serving the local specialities of cochonillo (suckling pig) and cordero asado (grilled lamb). **La Mesón Casa Cándido** *also offers a fine view of the aqueduct (Plaza del Azoguejo, 5 ☎ 92 181 02 03).*

PEDRAZA DE LA SIERRA

If you're touring by car, you could try this charming circular route from Madrid. Take the N1 as far as the junction with the N110 in the direction of Segovia. Stop for an aperitif in Plaza Mayor in Pedraza de la Sierra, a marvellous medieval village perched high over the surrounding countryside. If you want to have lunch in the country, continue on the N110 in the direction of Segovia as far as the 172km (108 mile) milestone. Although it's a little rustic, the **Molino de Río Viejo** *restaurant makes a charming setting, both indoors and out, but it's essential to book (☎ 921 40 30 63). Return by way of Segovia, which is about 30km (19 miles) away.*

NOTES

NOTES

NOTES

HACHETTE TRAVEL GUIDES

A GREAT WEEKEND IN ...

Amsterdam	1 84202 145 1
Barcelona	0 54008 323 2
Berlin	1 84202 061 7
Brussels	1 84202 017 X
Budapest	0 54008 274 0
Dublin	1 84202 096 X
Florence	0 54008 322 4
Lisbon	1 84202 011 0
London	1 84202 168 0
Madrid	1 84202 095 1
Naples	1 84202 016 1
New York	0 54008 321 6
Paris	1 84202 001 3
Prague	1 84202 000 5
Rome	1 84202 169 9
Seville	0 54008 275 9
Venice	1 84202 018 8
Stockholm	0 54008 318 6
Vienna	1 84202 026 9

ROUTARD

Indulge your taste for travel with the ultimate food, drink and accommodation guides for the independent traveller.

Andalucia & Southern Spain	1 84202 028 5
Athens & the Greek Islands	1 84202 023 4
Belgium	1 84202 022 6
North Brittany	1 84202 020 X
California, Nevada & Arizona	1 84202 025 0
Canada	1 84202 031 5
Cuba	1 84202 062 5
Ireland	1 84202 024 2
Paris	1 84202 027 7
Provence & the Côte d'Azur	1 84202 019 6
Rome & Southern Italy	1 84202 021 8
Thailand	1 84202 029 3

VACANCES

Colourful, information-packed, leisure and activity guides. Hundreds of suggestions for things to do and sights to see.

Alsace	1 84202 167 2
The Ardèche	1 84202 161 3
The Basque Country	1 84202 159 1
Brittany	1 84202 007 2
Catalonia	1 84202 099 4
Corsica	1 84202 100 1
The Dordogne & Périgord	1 84202 098 6
French Alps	1 84202 166 4
Languedoc-Roussillon	1 84202 008 0
Normandy	1 84202 097 8
Poitou-Charentes	1 84202 009 9
Provence & the Côte d'Azur	1 84202 006 4
Pyrenees & Gascony	1 84202 015 3
South West France	1 84202 014 5